Evaluations of Alternative Approaches to Central Stock Leveling

Louis W. Miller

John B. Abell

Prepared for the
United States Air Force

RAND

Project AIR FORCE

This report describes evaluations of several alternative approaches to the problem of setting stock levels at bases and depots for aircraft recoverable spare parts. A fixed safety level policy, somewhat akin to the procedure used by the Standard Base Supply System, is included along with the multi-echelon method used in AFMC's Central Stock Leveling System, known as D028, an implementation of METRIC (Multi-Echelon Technique for Recoverable Item Control).

Of special interest here is the performance of DRIVE (Distribution and Repair in Variable Environments), a computer-based decision support system originally intended to prioritize the depot-level repair and allocation of aircraft recoverable components. In this report, the extension of DRIVE's optimization algorithm to central stock leveling is discussed and evaluated.

This work was done in the Logistics Project, part of the Resource Management and System Acquisition Program of RAND's Project AIR FORCE. It was sponsored by the DCS/Logistics, Headquarters, USAF. It should be of interest to logisticians in all of the military departments and the Office of the Secretary of Defense, especially those concerned with supply policy and logistics research and analysis.

PROJECT AIR FORCE

Project AIR FORCE, a division of RAND, is the Air Force federally funded research and development center (FFRDC) for studies and analyses. It provides the Air Force with independent analyses of policy alternatives affecting the development, employment, combat readiness, and support of current and future aerospace forces. Research is being performed in three programs: Strategy, Doctrine, and Force Structure; Force Modernization and Employment; and Resource Management and System Acquisition.

CONTENTS

FIGURES

The principal conclusion of this research is that the Air Force should use DRIVE (Distribution and Repair in Variable Environments) in a desktop environment for central stock leveling, but only when it is used in execution to prioritize component repairs and allocate serviceable assets. We define central stock leveling as the determination of stock levels by a central authority with a view of all the users of a stock number in the logistics system, typically at an air logistics center, but not at each individual base. The term *desktop environment* implies the use of *Desktop DRIVE*, a PC-based implementation of DRIVE developed by the Dynamics Research Corporation. We found that this approach determines stock levels that perform as well as those of any of the well-known optimization models currently in use, either for determining aircraft recoverable spares requirements or central stock leveling, and that it will provide consistency between asset allocations recommended by Desktop DRIVE in execution and base due-ins.

We and others have observed that DRIVE in execution (prioritizing repairs and recommending asset allocations) sometimes recommends asset allocations to bases where there is no due-in and sometimes ignores requisitions in the depot backorder file for extended periods of time. These inconsistencies are induced by the fact that DRIVE ignores both stock levels and requisitions in its prioritization of repairs and allocation of serviceable assets to bases and the fact that it will not allocate an asset to a base without a due-in at that base.

Although the consistency between DRIVE's recommended asset allocations and base due-ins may seem to be an administrative formality, it is nontrivial in the sense that, with DRIVE in execution, one does not wish to have those recommended allocations inhibited by lack of a due-in at a base and, conversely, one does not want unfilled requisitions in the depot backorder file for long periods.

We hypothesized that such inconsistencies could be minimized by allocating stock levels using an adaptation of DRIVE that incorporated its underlying logic, and the stock levels thus produced would deliver better system performance than current stock leveling methods. After extensive evaluations, we concluded that the use of DRIVE for central stock leveling is a practical idea that not only resolves the problem of inconsistencies in asset allocations relative to base due-ins but also delivers as good as or better system performance than other methods. It is important, however, that DRIVE be used in execution (repair requirements, repair prioritization, and asset allocation) when it is used to determine stock levels.

The adaptation of DRIVE's underlying logic to the problem of determining stock levels is straightforward; in fact, we constructed such an adaptation in the course of this work to compare DRIVE with other approaches to central leveling. The vehicle of choice is Desktop DRIVE in its quarterly repair requirements determination mode. The scope of the stock leveling problem should be constrained to some fairly homogeneous set of NSNs being repaired in one or a few related shops. The Ogden F-16 avionics repair setting is a nearly perfect model of such an environment. Periodically, say quarterly, or whenever there is a change in the force beddown, flying hour program, mix of aircraft among bases, or other important factor, DRIVE would be run to recompute the stock levels for both LRUs (line-replaceable units) and SRUs (shop-replaceable units).

In determining quarterly repair requirements, budgetary and repair capacity constraints are applied to DRIVE's globally optimized, sequenced list of repair actions. Carcass constraints, of course, are already built into the list. This procedure is logically equivalent to applying the more constraining of a specified sort value and a carcass constraint to individual LRU families as a stopping rule; it yields the best mix of levels relative to other methods such as optimizing the geometric mean of the base probabilities. This approach has been used at Ogden for several years to determine quarterly repair requirements for F-16 avionics LRUs and SRUs.

Setting levels with DRIVE requires very little further development. Running DRIVE in its quarterly repair requirements mode enables one to estimate the end-of-quarter asset position that translates directly into stock levels.

When DRIVE is not used in execution, it should not be used to determine stock levels. In that case, AFMC's Central Stock Leveling System, D028, may be the approach of choice. D028 may have data or data processing problems we do not understand that could inhibit its effectiveness; nevertheless, as an implementation of METRIC (Multi-Echelon Technique for Recoverable Item Control), which we evaluated extensively in this work, its underlying logic is sound, at least for LRUs, and it is difficult to achieve better system performance than METRIC does in central LRU stock leveling. We cannot comment on its performance with SRUs because SRUs were excluded from this research in the interest of timeliness and simplicity. It is important that whatever problems may exist in implementing D028 for central stock leveling be resolved and that D028 again be made a viable system. For determining stock levels, it is clearly superior to the Standard Base Supply System and other approaches that do not have a view of all users of a stock number in the total system.

RESEARCH APPROACH

Although we were especially interested in the relative performance of D028 and DRIVE for central stock leveling, we evaluated other approaches as well, most notably the Aircraft Availability Model. We used Dyna-METRIC Version 6, modified to include a representation of DRIVE in execution, for the evaluations (Isaacson and Boren, 1993). Our principal evaluation scenario comprised two weapon systems, six bases, and 135 LRUs. Other scenarios were also explored, including the Air Force's B-1B weapon system.

GOALS, OBJECTIVE FUNCTIONS, AND PERFORMANCE MEASURES

When optimization models such as METRIC, the AAM, or DRIVE are used to determine stock levels using a systemwide objective function such as total expected backorders in the system or worldwide expected aircraft availability, they typically yield results that deliver heterogeneous levels of performance among bases and weapon systems. They tend to favor large bases over smaller ones and simpler weapon systems over more complex ones (where complexity is measured in terms of the number of LRUs that make up the system). Our results suggest that such heterogeneity is sufficiently large that in any resource allocation process involving prioritizations of actions for or allocations to individual bases, the effects of base size and weapon system complexity should be explicitly accounted for.

The overarching objective of the logistics system at large is to deliver specified levels of weapon system availability at least cost. Having said this, however, we hasten to add that, given the propensity for normative decisionmaking models operating within large data and management systems to favor simple weapon systems over complex ones and larger bases over smaller ones, weapon system availability goals must be specified by weapon system–base combination. Without explicit consideration of base-specific and weapon-system-specific goals, a normative model may yield levels of performance that are, as a practical matter, unacceptable to military commanders. We explore this topic at greater length in the body of this report.

THE CASE FOR CENTRAL STOCK LEVELING

When the stock levels for a particular item are determined centrally and allocated to the bases, their sum can be constrained to equal the total number of assets of that type in the inventory system. This constraint has the important advantage of limiting the number of requisitions in the system to the assets available. If the stock leveling mechanism does not allocate more stock levels of an item than is consistent with the optimization of a weapon system availability objective function, and also does not allocate stock levels beyond the number of assets in the system, it will minimize the number of unfilled requisitions and will not allocate stock levels for assets whose repair and allocation are not likely to eventuate. The stock levels can then be used as production constraints for depot repair.

As we pointed out previously, a sensible balance between base due-ins and asset allocation recommendations is not just an administrative nicety. It substantially shapes people's perceptions of depot performance.

ANOTHER KEY OBSERVATION

This work may have important implications for the Air Force's "lean logistics" concept of operations. With DRIVE determining stock levels and operating in execution with a very responsive depot repair and transportation/distribution system, it is possible to achieve levels of system performance that are roughly equivalent to those hypothesized for the buffer stock arrangement (the equivalent of depot stock in our terms) of the lean logistics concept. Why, then, should one pay the price of storage and management of buffer stock? An alternative supply system configuration with DRIVE used in execution and central stock leveling may deliver equal performance at less cost.

RECOMMENDATIONS

Our recommendations are few and straightforward. First, we recommend the use of DRIVE for central stock leveling, but only when DRIVE is used in repair prioritization and asset allocation. It should be implemented using Desktop DRIVE and its use should be demonstrated in stock leveling at Ogden for F-16 avionics components.

The use of the SBSS and negotiated stock levels should be avoided whenever possible. D028 is, in principle, a superior method of setting stock levels. When DRIVE is not used in execution, D028 is clearly the approach of choice. The problems inhibiting the use of D028 should be resolved and it should be made fully operational again.

This research should be extended to include SRUs. Moreover, additional research is needed in setting aircraft availability goals with DRIVE, both in stock leveling and in execution, and should include extensive evaluations of system performance, especially when DRIVE is used to set differential goals. Incorporation of an expected aircraft availability objective function in DRIVE should also be fully developed.

ACKNOWLEDGMENTS

We are indebted to our colleagues at RAND: Ms. Karen Isaacson, for helping modify Dyna-METRIC to accommodate DRIVE in execution; Ms. Mary Chenoweth, for her assistance with Dyna-METRIC and computer programming; and Dr. Lionel Galway, for his assistance with the bootstrapping methods we used to understand the problem of estimating error variance. Mr. Bob McCormick, Headquarters, AFMC/XPSA, kindly provided the B-1B data used in our analyses. Dr. Christopher Hanks, Dr. Kenneth Girardini, and Dr. Frank Camm provided very helpful, constructive reviews of the manuscript.

Chapter One

INTRODUCTION

In 1987, the Ogden Air Logistics Center successfully demonstrated the feasibility of the idea of using a computer-based decision support system called DRIVE (Distribution and Repair in Variable Environments) to prioritize the repair of aircraft recoverable[1] components and allocate the serviceable assets emerging from repair to Air Force bases worldwide. DRIVE suggests repair and allocation sequences that approximately maximize the probability of achieving specified aircraft availability goals at all the bases in the face of a repair capacity constraint (Abell et al., 1992; Miller and Abell, 1992). Following that initial demonstration, the Air Force Materiel Command (then the Air Force Logistics Command) decided to develop a production version of the prototype system demonstrated at Ogden. In the months following the prototype demonstration, we modified DRIVE and applied it to the problem of determining quarterly repair requirements. After several intervening years, DRIVE was implemented as a PC-based system called Desktop DRIVE.[2] Desktop DRIVE is currently in use at Ogden, not only for prioritizing component repairs and determining quarterly repair requirements, but also for allocating serviceable components to bases through automated inputs to the Air Force's Stock Control and Distribution System (D035).

Before the implementation of these automated inputs, we and others involved in this system development observed that DRIVE would sometimes recommend the allocation of an asset to a base when there was no due-in for the asset at that base.[3] Another, similar disconnect sometimes arose in the form of a backorder that remained unfilled for a long period. These inconsistencies be-

---

[1]A *recoverable* component is one that is subject to repair when it fails, as distinguished from a *consumable*, which is discarded upon failure or consumed in use.

[2]Desktop DRIVE was developed by the Dynamics Research Corporation.

[3]A *due-in* is an unfilled requisition. A due-in exists if a requisition has not yet been filled by the source of supply (a depot backorder) or if the asset has been shipped by the source of supply but has not yet been received by the base (an in-transit serviceable). Due-ins from maintenance at the base (DIFM) are ignored here.

tween DRIVE's recommended allocations and base due-ins were obviously a cause of concern even though independent evaluations had judged DRIVE's performance superior to that of the current system (Culosi and Eichorn, 1993).

STOCK LEVELS AND RECOVERABLE ITEM MANAGEMENT

Actually, there is no reason why DRIVE's recommended allocations and base due-ins should match perfectly. DRIVE's underlying logic is that of a push system. It recommends asset allocations on the basis of expected demands, aircraft availability goals, and the current worldwide asset position, i.e., the asset position at each base and the depot. It ignores both stock levels and requisitions in its recommendations, but in practice no asset is shipped to a base unless a due-in exists for the asset at that base.

The Air Force supply system is a pull system, i.e., it allocates assets to requisitions using priorities specified by MILSTRIP (military standard requisitioning and issue procedures). Underlying the submission of requisitions is a *reorder policy* implemented through *stock levels*. Each Air Force base generates requisitions for recoverable assets using an $(S, S-1)$ reorder policy (where S denotes the stock level), i.e., *a continuous review policy with an order quantity of one.* Whenever the number of assets of a particular type on hand (OH), plus the number due in (DI), minus the number due out to maintenance at the base (DO), falls below the stock level (S), the base immediately submits a requisition to the source of supply for a replacement asset. Thus, the stock level is a number that shapes reorder behavior; it is not an inventory position. The order quantity on requisitions for aircraft recoverable spare parts is one about 97 percent of the time.

We formally define a stock level as

$$S = OH + DI - DO. \tag{1}$$

From the preceding paragraph, the stock level is equal to assets on hand plus due-ins minus due-outs. We can rewrite the above relationship to define due-ins as

$$DI = S - (OH - DO). \tag{2}$$

Again, for purposes of clarification, we define an asset position, AP, as the number of assets on hand including due-outs, which can be thought of as negative assets, i.e., under normal procedures, the base supply account cannot have a due-out unless there is no stock on hand; thus, OH and DO cannot both be positive. Thus, we define

$$AP = OH - DO; \tag{3}$$

note that AP will be negative when the base has one or more due-outs. If we substitute this definition in (2) above, we have

$$DI = S - AP. \tag{4}$$

This equation should make the difference between stock level and asset position clear. The stock level is a policy variable that shapes reorder behavior; the asset position describes actual inventory status. The foregoing discussion, especially equation (4), should also make clear why stock levels set by approaches other than DRIVE induce differences between base due-ins and DRIVE's recommended asset allocations. The number of due-ins is determined by both the stock level and the asset position. If the stock level for a particular item is lower than the level that would have been set by DRIVE operating in a stock-leveling mode, DRIVE may suggest allocating an asset for which there is no due-in. Similarly, if a stock level is higher than a stock-leveling version of DRIVE would have established, DRIVE may never try to fill the resulting backorder(s).

Stock levels that sum to the total number of assets in the inventory system worldwide determine the richness of asset positions at bases relative to other bases and the richness of stocks of particular line-replaceable units (LRUs) relative to other LRUs. Because DRIVE ignores stock levels in allocating assets, it really has no stopping rule in its asset allocation algorithm. Given any set of serviceable assets, it will invariably allocate next the asset that will do the combat force the most good in terms of its availability goals.

If, on the other hand, DRIVE sets the stock levels for the items and bases involved, and it is programmed to remember its stopping rule, it will not recommend asset allocations beyond the stock levels it sets; nor will it indefinitely ignore backorders that result from asset positions below the corresponding stock levels unless it is constrained by repair capacity.

STOCK LEVELING IN THE CURRENT SYSTEM

In the current system, stock levels for recoverable aircraft spare parts have typically been determined in one of three ways: (a) by AFMC's Central Stock Leveling System (D028), (b) by the Air Force's Standard Base Supply System (SBSS), or (c) by negotiation between the base and the item manager. They are infrequently set through other processes that won't be discussed here. D028 and the SBSS use different criteria in setting stock levels. The SBSS develops stock levels at a base on the basis of past demand without regard for the total numbers of assets in the inventory system and without visibility of other bases. It does not make tradeoffs among bases, items, or weapon systems, and its stock levels may be quite inconsistent with the assets available.

D028, on the other hand, develops stock levels intended to minimize total expected base-level backorders in the system. It has visibility of the number of assets of each type that D041 (the Air Force's requirements determination system for aircraft recoverable spares, known officially as the *Recoverable Consumption Item Requirements System*) wants to see in the inventory system five quarters beyond the buy point. Thus, D028 is able to constrain the sum of its stock levels to the total numbers of assets in the inventory system or that are intended to be in the inventory system at some future time.[4] As one would expect, the stock levels that emerge from the SBSS and D028 are often different.

Negotiated levels seem to be used most often to establish stock levels that would not otherwise exist. For our purposes here, it is important to note that, although the Air Force supply system is a pull system, D028 computes stock levels centrally and "pushes" the levels to the bases, in contrast to the SBSS, with which each base computes its own levels. When D028 establishes a stock level, it overrides any stock level set by the SBSS.

Backorders in the system may need to be adjusted whenever stock levels change, as they do periodically (quarterly in the case of D028). If a stock level increases, for example, a base may need to submit one or more requisitions to cover the increase. If a stock level decreases and there are backorders in the system, the base needs to cancel one or more of them to respond to the decrease. If there is no backorder in the system, one or more assets on hand will become excess to the base's requirement and may be reallocated.

OUR PRINCIPAL RESEARCH HYPOTHESIS

It should be clear from the foregoing discussion that the mix of backorders is determined in part by the mix of stock levels. Since stock levels are currently determined by methods that use different criteria than DRIVE uses to allocate assets, it is little wonder that DRIVE's recommended allocations are sometimes inconsistent with the backorders currently in the system.

When we first observed this inconsistency, we realized that DRIVE's logic could easily be extended to the problem of determining stock levels, and that DRIVE's recommended asset allocations would then be more consistent with the back-

---

[4]The future time may be as long as three years from the asset cutoff date, i.e., the date of the asset position that underlies the requirements computation. This has problems of its own (Hanks and Kline, 1987). For our research purposes, we assumed that the sum of the stock levels allocated equaled the total number of assets in the inventory system and that there were no assets acquired from procurement and no condemnations during the simulations.

order position, for the reasons we have already discussed. Applying DRIVE to the problem of determining stock levels is straightforward. During the course of this work we developed software modifications that extend DRIVE's application to stock leveling. Thus, the feasibility of the idea has already been demonstrated.

The remaining issue addressed in this research was to estimate the system performance delivered by alternative approaches to the central stock leveling problem. If D028 determines stock levels that deliver better performance than DRIVE's stock levels for the same total number of assets, it may not be prudent to change the approach simply for the sake of consistency. The principal thrust of the research discussed in this report is to examine this fundamental question by comparing the performance of the mix of stock levels determined by applying DRIVE to the stock leveling problem with the performance of other methods.

Toward that end, we evaluated several alternative approaches to central stock leveling, including two normative models used by the Air Force: METRIC (Multi-Echelon Technique for Recoverable Item Control) and the Aircraft Availability Model (AAM). D028 is essentially AFMC's implementation of METRIC, RAND's seminal work in multi-echelon inventory theory done in the 1960s (Sherbrooke, 1968). METRIC was first implemented by AFLC in 1975 to determine replenishment requirements for aircraft recoverable spares. It was replaced in that role in 1989 by the Aircraft Availability Model, developed by the Logistics Management Institute (O'Malley, 1983). For purposes of comparison, two versions of the AAM were included in our evaluations. We also examined a fixed-safety-level approach, which roughly represents the SBSS, and an approach that optimizes fill rate. The marginal costs of including these additional approaches in the evaluations were small, and the inclusion of the AAM, especially, yielded very useful information.

All of the approaches evaluated in this work depend on estimating item pipelines—except DRIVE. DRIVE ignores pipelines and is a distinctly different approach from all the others. Moreover, unlike METRIC and the AAM, it is not a multi-echelon model. It also makes different assumptions about cannibalization than METRIC and the AAM. We explain these and other differences later.

PERFORMANCE MEASURES

As our research progressed, it raised almost as many questions as it answered. Every alternative approach to determining stock levels has characteristics of its own. For example, the objective functions differ, as do the mechanisms underlying the marginal analytic operations among the several models. The mixes of stock levels determined by the various approaches also differ, sometimes quite dramatically, even when they deliver roughly the same performance when measured by an aircraft availability criterion.

The performance measure one uses to discriminate among the alternative approaches cannot be one-dimensional. There are several important criteria one must use to judge the performance of any particular approach, worldwide aircraft availability being only one of them. For example, does an approach tend to favor large bases at the expense of smaller ones, or small ones at the expense of larger ones? To what extent does it tend to favor less expensive items over more expensive ones? Does it tend to favor less complex aircraft at the expense of more complex ones (where we measure complexity in terms of the number of LRUs installed in an aircraft)? Does its performance hold up well without cannibalization or lateral supply?

These are some of the questions we faced as this research evolved. We discuss them at length in the chapters that follow. By way of introduction, we describe our general approach to this research and summarize our conclusions very briefly in the remainder of this chapter.

RESEARCH APPROACH

We define two problems, the requirements problem and the stock leveling problem, even though our principal interest is in the latter. The requirements problem is to determine a mix of stock levels with a specified total cost. The stock leveling problem is to allocate stock levels to locations in the logistics system such that the sum of the stock levels for each item equals the number of assets of that item in the inventory system; thus, the mix of assets in the system is predetermined and only their allocation remains to be decided by any particular approach. The bulk of our work evaluated alternative approaches using the requirements problem. The reason for this is that alternative approaches yielded more similar performance when the total numbers of assets of each type were fixed. We were able to discriminate somewhat better among the alternative approaches using the requirements problem.

It is important to note that, in adapting DRIVE to central stock leveling, one would typically solve neither the requirements problem nor the pure stock leveling problem. As a practical matter, one would solve a third problem that is something of a hybrid between the two because one would use DRIVE to allocate stock levels up to the number of assets in the inventory system or until additional stock levels would not yield significant contributions to aircraft availability. Thus, the mix of assets available is not always a constraint, as it is in the pure stock leveling problem.

To support our evaluations, we built a system of software that includes all of the stock leveling approaches of interest. For each approach, the software system computed the stock levels and wrote an input database for evaluation by Dyna-METRIC Version 6 (Isaacson and Boren, 1993).[5] Using Dyna-METRIC, we were able to evaluate the alternative approaches in several different ways, as we explain in later chapters. We also made an important modification to Dyna-METRIC through the addition of DRIVE as an execution system. We were able to run Dyna-METRIC with and without DRIVE activated, and drew an important conclusion from that ability.

We examined the performance of the alternative approaches using several scenarios, but finally decided to discuss one particular scenario at length. It comprises six bases, 135 LRUs, and two weapon systems. The characteristics of the LRUs, such as demand rate, NRTS rate, and cost, were specified by us. We also evaluated the alternatives using real-world B-1B aircraft data. We examined two other scenarios as well, one with fewer LRUs and one with more bases. We describe other details of the scenarios in our discussions of issues and results.

OVERALL CONCLUSION

The important overall conclusion we reached in this research is that the Air Force should extend the use of DRIVE to determine stock levels in lieu of D028 or the SBSS, but only when it is using DRIVE to prioritize repairs and allocate assets. We will say much more about this and our other observations and conclusions in later chapters.

WHAT FOLLOWS

In Chapter Two, we discuss the roles of goals, objective functions, and performance measures in several important logistics processes associated with aircraft recoverable spares, including the stock leveling process. In Chapter Three, we discuss alternative stock leveling methods, their characteristics, and issues raised by their use. Each of these methods shares the common characteristic of an item pipeline computation. We discuss DRIVE in Chapter Four, pointing out how and why it differs from the more traditional pipeline approaches, and the issues raised by its use. In Chapters Five, Six, and Seven, we present and discuss the results of our evaluations. We summarize our conclusions and recommendations in Chapter Eight.

---

[5]Version 6 is the latest, most advanced version of Dyna-METRIC, the Air Force's standard capability assessment model developed by RAND.

Chapter Two

GOALS, OBJECTIVE FUNCTIONS, AND PERFORMANCE MEASURES IN CENTRAL STOCK LEVELING

What we mean by *central stock leveling* is the determination of stock levels by some central authority, typically an air logistics center, or perhaps less desirably a major command headquarters, but not by each individual base. We do not imply that all stock levels in the system are determined by a single agent; in fact, we prefer an implementation of central stock leveling that is distributed among air logistics centers where the actual operations are carried out in desktop environments with sufficiently modest scope to allow human intervention and tractable coordination in the process.

This research in central stock leveling raises several issues that have important implications for other processes in the logistics system. In the discussion that follows, we explore some of these issues, primarily in the context of central stock leveling, but also in the context of other processes involved in delivering aircraft recoverable spare parts when and where needed. We limit our discussion to aircraft recoverable parts.

We define the achievement of specified aircraft availability goals at least total systemwide cost to be the most desirable overarching objective of all the functional entities and processes involved in recoverable spares management.

The characteristics of any normative computer-based algorithms that are applied on a large scale (e.g., to many parts, many bases, many weapon systems) are of special interest in logistics processes because they tend to shape the cost-effectiveness of the process and, therefore, of the logistics system. That is the case in stock leveling, although, as we will show in later chapters, system performance is less sensitive to alternative approaches to stock leveling than to decisionmaking in certain other logistics processes.

As we pointed out in Chapter One, the vast majority of stock levels in the system are determined centrally by D028, locally by the SBSS, or are negotiated levels determined in a somewhat ad hoc process involving the item manager and the base supply activity. D028 allocates stock levels to locations worldwide. As we pointed out in Chapter One, it is the Air Force's implementation of METRIC applied to the stock leveling problem. Assets are allocated against the stock levels through MILSTRIP, i.e., through requisitions submitted by base supply to the source of supply. Given adequate data, central leveling allows the Air Force to set stock levels in a more nearly optimal way than if stock levels are determined locally. Moreover, the central stock leveling process can take explicit account of the total number of assets in the inventory system and allocate levels so that, in most cases, the sum of the levels equals the total number of assets, thus avoiding both unallocated assets and unfilled requisitions.[1]

The notion of optimality implies an objective function, i.e., some measure of process performance whose maximization or minimization subject to some constraint is of principal interest in the stock leveling process. The choice of objective function is seldom trivial in systems as complicated as the Air Force logistics system. In the case of automated systems that deal with complex problems, the choice is typically constrained by mathematical tractability. Examples of objective functions in the stock leveling problem include fill rates, total expected base-level backorders in the system, worldwide aircraft availability, and the probability of achieving specified aircraft availability goals at all the bases.

The traditional versions of each of the three most important optimization algorithms evaluated in this research, METRIC, the AAM, and DRIVE, use objective functions that are specific to systemwide performance; in DRIVE's case, however, availability goals are specified by weapon system and base combination. Each algorithm has characteristics that yield differential performance by base size (number of aircraft at a base) and weapon system complexity, where we define *complexity* in terms of the number of LRUs in the weapon system. METRIC, for example, tends to allocate stock levels that favor large bases over smaller ones and simple aircraft over more complex ones. The same is true for the AAM. DRIVE favors large bases over smaller ones to a lesser extent, but also favors simpler aircraft over more complex ones.

As a result of such characteristics, one cannot compare alternative approaches to stock leveling on the basis of worldwide aircraft availability alone; one needs a richer, multidimensional measure of performance that reflects base-specific and weapon-system-specific availability. When we examine the aircraft availability at each base in a scenario, we see differential levels of performance that may be important to the Air Force. They may imply unacceptable availability for, say, the C-5 aircraft, which has many LRUs, and greater availability than needed for some simpler aircraft. They may also imply undesirably lower availability rates within a weapon system at smaller bases than larger ones.

---

[1] For a more definitive discussion, see Hanks and Kline (1987).

GOAL SETTING

If, when asked to specify an availability goal for, say, the F-16 aircraft, a decisionmaker says "85 percent" in the belief that he is specifying 85 percent for every base, then the stock leveling algorithm needs to be constrained to do that. If left unconstrained, METRIC, the AAM, and DRIVE will each allocate stock levels that yield distinctly different levels of performance among bases, depending on their sizes.

We hasten to add that the AAM comprises computer algorithms other than the one that computes the spares requirement. These programs enable a decisionmaker to specify aircraft availability goals by weapon system and allocate the costs for common components among the weapon systems to which they apply. Thus, it is possible to allocate a spares budget across weapon systems with the AAM in a way that may improve the mix of aircraft availabilities.

Ultimately, one might argue that an optimization model really should focus on a worldwide objective function, which we tend to think of as the systemwide objective. Our argument is that although the globally optimal solution may very well be the preferred one, the decisionmaker should understand exactly what his choice implies for every unit commander and weapon system at every location, and that those implications be carefully considered in the choice of objective function, the formulation of constraints in the optimization algorithm, and the setting of goals.

Aircraft availability goals not only affect priorities among weapon systems and bases, but also imply budgetary levels in processes in which costs are a consideration. Although cost constraints are not applicable to the stock leveling problem per se, they do apply to other processes involved with aircraft recoverable spares. Because an optimization model can determine the budget required for any set of goals, it can be very helpful in goal setting. If goals or cost constraints are specified independent of the optimization model, they may be inconsistent with each other. If the cost constraint is too severe, the goals may not be met. If the goals are too high, there may not be sufficient funding available to meet them. The budgetary requirement is tied inextricably to the set of specified goals; each implies the other once the optimization model and constraints have been specified. The specification of a budgetary constraint sometimes implies judgments about what levels of performance are adequate and sometimes about what levels of performance are affordable. The actual solution will depend on which specification stops the optimization, reaching the goal or the budgetary constraint.

Another issue must be faced in goal setting that may be somewhat troublesome technically: the numerical values of goals may have to be tailored to the particular algorithm used. DRIVE, for example, has an objective function whose numerical value is small, i.e., the probability of meeting aircraft availability goals at all the bases. The AAM is known to underestimate aircraft availability; its estimates need to be adjusted upwards. A complicating problem is that it uses an average base assumption, i.e., it assumes that all the bases in the system look alike. As we show in later chapters, METRIC doesn't explicitly consider aircraft availability. In its implementation as VSL (Variable Safety Level), the Air Force's former method for computing requirements for safety stock in D041, its investment levels were shaped by the use of Lagrangian multipliers, a rather tedious and cumbersome process.

OBJECTIVE FUNCTIONS AND PERFORMANCE MEASURES

The choice of objective functions is often shaped by mathematical tractability. Tradeoffs may be involved between the objective function and other character-istics of the algorithm, for example its treatment of indenture levels. METRIC, for example, treats SRUs (shop-replaceable units) like LRUs; a shortage of an SRU is viewed to be as serious as that of an LRU. In estimating expected back-orders for SRUs, the AAM makes the unfortunate assumption that every SRU shortage holds down an LRU, which implies that no LRU can have multiple SRU failures. Neither approach deals with cannibalization. DRIVE, on the other hand, although providing a reasonable treatment of the indenture relationship and cannibalization, has a rather unfortunate objective function. Thus, opti-mization models are not always genuinely optimal in complicated problems. In other words, a model's objective function and assumptions may not be well re-lated to the real world. Moreover, as we pointed out already, they often have characteristics that are not clearly understood by users, decisionmakers, and policymakers in the logistics system.

In this research we evaluated several stock leveling approaches using a capabil-ity assessment model exogenous to the stock leveling process to achieve a more objective evaluation of alternative approaches. Although our principal perfor-mance measure was aircraft availability, we also examined the probability of achieving the aircraft availability goals at all bases as another measure of per-formance. These measures suggested somewhat different preferences. When comparing the performance of several approaches, each of which uses a differ-ent objective function, it is important that a natural performance measure of each approach be included in the evaluation. By this we simply mean that in comparing an approach that maximizes fill rate, for example, with one that maximizes aircraft availability, one should not evaluate them with a fill rate measure alone.

CENTRAL STOCK LEVELING

There are several compelling arguments in favor of central stock leveling over local approaches at bases. First, it is desirable to have the sum of the stock levels at all locations equal the total number of spares in the system. The only way to ensure that this condition is met is to set the stock levels centrally and allocate them to the bases. If this is not done, the richness of stock levels at the bases may far exceed the assets available. Second, although it might be possible to compute a set of stock levels locally that is "optimal" for that specific base (in the form of a requirements problem) when item characteristics are known and aircraft availability goals are specified for all weapon systems at the base, the SBSS is unable to do this using its current stock leveling approach. The SBSS approach is demand based and item specific, i.e., it does not make tradeoffs among items and it takes no account of weapon systems or availability goals. Third, locally computed stock levels need more than local data to avoid undesirable instability in statistical estimates of item characteristics; there are problems associated with using base-specific data alone to estimate certain item characteristics, the best example of which is the item NRTS rate (the percentage of repairable generations that are declared "not repairable this station"). Worldwide data are also needed for such estimates, which implies, again, a central computation.[2]

All these considerations apply equally well to negotiated levels. Given the overarching system objective of achieving specified aircraft availability goals at least cost, SBSS levels and negotiated levels should be avoided except in extraordinary circumstances. With reliable data systems, a central leveling approach is clearly superior.

IMPLICATIONS FOR OTHER LOGISTICS PROCESSES

The findings of this work, although perhaps not surprising to many in the logistics research community, may illuminate the policy choices the Air Force faces in goal setting and in constraining the computer-based algorithms that underlie the automated decisionmaking that occurs in several of the logistics processes associated with aircraft recoverable spares, stock leveling among them.

The same overarching goal of achieving specified availability goals at least cost applies to each of the following processes:

- Determining spares investment levels and mixes of requirements

- Buying spares (execution)

---

[2]Although D028 is a central computation, it does not take full advantage of worldwide data.

- Stock leveling

- Allocating assets (execution)

- Determining repair requirements over quarterly and longer planning horizons

- Prioritizing repairs (execution)

DRIVE is already used to support the last three of these processes and, we conclude, should be used for stock leveling whenever it is being used for asset allocation. It seems unlikely that, lacking a pipeline computation, DRIVE should ever be used for determining spares investment levels or computing spares requirements.

Chapter Three

PIPELINE MODELS

This chapter reviews the normative "pipeline" models for requirements determination and allocating stock levels that were considered in this study. These include *fill rate, fixed safety level, METRIC (and VARI-METRIC)*, and the *Aircraft Availability Model*. The models have much in common; they share the same abstract view of the logistics system and set of assumptions. We begin by discussing the common aspects of pipeline models and end by describing the specifics pertaining to the various models. The differences are mainly attributable to their individual objective functions.

THE LOGISTICS WORLD ACCORDING TO PIPELINE MODELS

Figure 3.1 diagrams the flow of parts from removal from aircraft on the flightline, through a network of pipelines (indicated by cylinders) and stockage points (indicated by boxes), to installation back in airplanes. The totality of stock levels determined by any of the models is equal to the total number of parts in the system beyond those needed to equip all aircraft. During operation we expect to find parts in pipelines, and therefore the number of serviceable parts on hand at any stockage point will normally be less than the stock level.

Objective Functions

The payoff, of course, is at the flightline, and our concern is for parts missing from airplanes due to there being no serviceable replacements in base supply. This concern is reflected in different ways by the objective functions associated with the various stock leveling procedures. Fill rate models seek to maximize the likelihood that a replacement part is available in base supply at the moment it is needed on the flightline. Although relatively easy to measure in execution, fill rate maximization is not a particularly good basis for allocating stock levels because it does not take into account *how long* part shortages persist. Fixed safety level models do try to control values of time-weighted stockouts, but they fail to recognize the interaction between depot and base stock levels, and they

RAND*MR546-3.1*

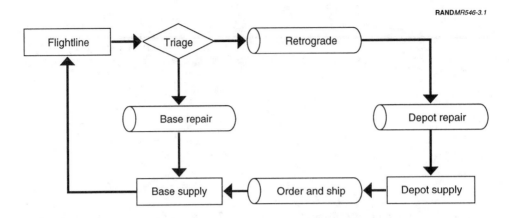

Figure 3.1—Flow of Parts in Pipeline Models

do not account for cost differences among parts in requirements determination applications. METRIC, which minimizes total expected time-weighted backorders over all parts at all bases, remedies these defects. Total expected backorders, however, is not aircraft availability. The Aircraft Availability Model uses METRIC's calculation but goes beyond by turning expected backorders into the probability that an airplane selected at random has no missing parts.

Removals and Triage

Pipeline models assume that the removals of any kind of part at a particular base are a Poisson process[1] that depends on an average removal rate. (Estimating removal rates is an important problem in the application of any stock leveling model, but we are assuming in this discussion that demand rates are available as data.) The diamond labeled "triage" in Figure 3.1 represents the decision that a part should be repaired either at the base or the depot, depending on the base's capability for dealing with the problem. The models assume that the selections between base and depot repair are independent random events. (This may not be true when, for example, parts are sent to the depot because a critical piece of test equipment at a base is temporarily unavailable.)

---

[1]This means that the number of parts removed in a fixed time interval is a random variable that has a Poisson probability distribution. Poisson random variables have variances equal to their means. Poisson processes result from the assumptions that the rate at which events occur is constant over time and that numbers of events in two disjoint time periods are statistically independent. The theory underlying pipeline models holds up under compounding, which allows consideration of processes where the variance exceeds the mean, with the negative binomial distribution being a popular example. It is also possible to drop the constant rate assumption, which is the basis of the analytic version of Dyna-METRIC and other models used in non-steady-state analyses.

The probability that a part goes to the higher echelon is called the *NRTS rate* for "not repairable this station."

Pipelines

The four cylindrical objects in Figure 3.1 are the pipelines representing base repair, retrograde from base to depot, depot repair, and the time required for a part to be ordered and shipped from the depot assuming that a part is available in depot supply. The crucial assumption is that the time spent by a part in a pipeline is a random variable that is independent of how many total parts are in the pipeline. This "infinite server" assumption is plausible for the retrograde and order-and-ship pipelines, but may be problematic for the two repair pipelines. If repair capacity is constrained, for example by a limited number of test stands, queues would form, and this might not be a very good model.[2]

The infinite server assumption plays in the following way. The assumption of Poisson removals propagates through the whole network so that the entrance of parts into any of the pipelines is also a Poisson process. This permits the application of Palm's Theorem that says that the steady-state probability distribution for the number of parts in a pipeline is a Poisson distribution whose mean is the arrival rate of parts into the pipeline multiplied by the average time that parts stay in the pipeline (Palm, 1938). What is remarkable is that the *form* of the distribution of the time spent by parts in a pipeline is not important; all we need to know is the mean. This implies that given only the rate, say parts per day, at which parts flow through a pipeline and the mean time spent in the pipeline, we know the entire probability distribution of the number of parts in the pipeline.

Supply Points

The operation of base supply and depot supply is straightforward. In the case of base supply, at the time of a part removal, a part is immediately handed over to base maintenance for installation in an aircraft if there are any serviceables on hand. Otherwise, one or more backorders exist awaiting replenishment from either base repair or the order-and-ship pipeline. In the case of depot supply, a base that sends a part to the depot simultaneously requisitions one from the depot. If there is a serviceable part in depot supply, the part is immediately put into the order-and-ship pipeline to the base. If not, the base suffers an additional wait for a part to emerge from the depot repair pipeline. In that

---

[2]This is one reason why a Monte Carlo simulation version of Dyna-METRIC was developed. Unfortunately, the simulation model can only be used descriptively for capability assessments and not normatively for setting stock levels.

event, the time between placement of the requisition and the replacement part entering the order-and-ship pipeline is the sum of the retrograde and depot repair times. Palm's Theorem applies to the number of requisitions delayed in this way.

Number in Resupply

When stock levels are specified, the assumptions we have made are sufficient to permit the calculation of the steady-state probability distributions of the number of parts in resupply (due-ins) to base supply. There is a separate distribution for each part at each base. These distributions are taken to be either of the Poisson form or a closely related distribution. All the models under discussion utilize the distributions of parts in resupply but differ in how they employ the distributions in optimizing their respective objective functions.

Multi-Echelon Models

Stock leveling procedures may differ on how they treat the network depicted in Figure 3.1. The main issue is whether or not they are multi-echelon computations. A truly multi-echelon model recognizes and appropriately trades off the interaction between base and depot stocks. The more stock placed at a base, the more frequently will a part removed from an airplane be replaced without delay. In the absence of lateral supply, however, parts stocked at a base are usable only by that base. On the other hand, a part placed in depot stock would be available to all bases, but the part has to pass through the order-and-ship pipeline before a base that requisitions the part can have it.

These considerations lead to two intuitively appealing notions. If some kind of part is scarce, so that there are not enough to go around, it would be best to hold much of the available supply at the depot to see which bases will need the part. Conversely, if supplies are ample, it would be better to distribute parts to the bases where they would be readily available. The second notion relates to sensitivity to the order-and-ship pipeline. If it is very short, bases would suffer little additional delay if most stock were kept centrally. But if order-and-ship times are long, a better solution would be to distribute more parts to the bases to avoid long delays.

METRIC (Sherbrooke, 1968) was the seminal work in multi-echelon inventory theory. Any of the procedures discussed in this chapter can be based on METRIC's computation of the distribution of the number of parts in resupply. The Air Force's implementation of the fixed safety level model prior to the adoption of METRIC, however, was not multi-echelon, and our interpretation of fixed safety level corresponds to the original. Our version of the fill rate model is not based on any historical implementation, and our version does use the METRIC computation. VARI-METRIC (Sherbrooke, 1986) is an elaborated version of METRIC to approximately correct for an untrue assumption that METRIC makes.

OPTIMIZATION AND COPING WITH MULTIPLE DIMENSIONS

The preceding material relates to the probability models that stock leveling procedures use in evaluating their objective functions when the stock levels are specified. With the exception of our fixed safety level method, to make a stock leveling procedure complete, the probability model and objective function calculation need to be imbedded in an optimum-seeking procedure. Marginal analysis is a generally applicable and efficient method. The idea is to build up a solution by allocating parts one at a time. At each step the choice of a part added to a location is the allocation that gives the most "bang for the buck." In the requirements problem we want the best value of the objective function for the total value being invested in parts. Thus, the criterion for choosing an allocation at each step is the improvement in the objective function divided by the cost of the part.[3] These ratios are frequently called "sort values."

Marginal analysis has a second advantage in requirements problems. Decisionmakers generally are interested in the tradeoff between the objective function and budget. The step-by-step operation of marginal analysis permits the calculation of the efficient tradeoff function. The pure stock leveling problem is simpler. In that case, the numbers of parts of every kind are given as constraints. Therefore, costs are not relevant, and tradeoff curves are not required.

Marginal analysis is essentially a search procedure in which one is looking for the best move at each step. The fewer alternatives that need to be examined, the better. A full-blown multi-echelon model such as METRIC is inherently three-dimensional. The dimensions are bases, parts, and for each part, the amount of depot stock. Searching over all three dimensions simultaneously is not practical, and there needs to be a way to break down the optimization into a sequence of one-dimensional problems. Later we will show how this is done with METRIC and indicate the problem with the Aircraft Availability Model.

This ends our general discussion of pipeline models, and we now turn to the specifics of the individual procedures. We begin with fixed safety level and go

---

[3]Formally, these problems are to maximize or minimize a nonlinear objective function subject to a single constraint. Marginal analysis is proper if there is a single constraint and the objective function is expressible as a sum, where each term in the sum is related to one of the choices (e.g., one kind of part to one location). The individual terms must be convex (i.e., show decreasing marginal returns).

on to METRIC, VARI-METRIC, and varieties of the Aircraft Availability Model. The fill rate model will be described as a variation on METRIC.

FIXED SAFETY LEVEL (FSL)

FSL is obsolete, but we are interested in seeing how much better more modern procedures are. We used FSL as a way of determining total numbers of parts to use as constraints when comparing other procedures applied to pure stock leveling problems (figuring that it would be neither too smart nor too dumb).

Although FSL provides for both depot and base stock levels, it is not truly multi-echelon because the two kinds of stock are calculated independently. Moreover, FSL does not have an optimization component that is characteristic of later methods. Depot stock levels are simple days-of-supply computations. That is, for each part, multiply the daily arrival rate of broken parts to the depot by some number of days. (As applied by the Air Force, the number of days was either 15 or 30, depending on the cost of the part.)

For base stocks, the stock level is determined by multiplying the standard deviation of the number of parts in resupply by a "safety factor." Think of a stock level as being a number of extra parts placed at the base beyond those needed for the aircraft. The net number of spare parts on hand is the stock level minus the number in resupply, a figure we do not want to go negative. The idea behind the calculation is to provide the base with enough spare parts so that the probability that the base does not run out of parts is at least equal to a specified value.

To estimate the standard deviation of the number of parts in resupply, an expected delay is computed as the sum of the expected depot-to-base order-and-ship time and an average base repair time, weighted by the NRTS rate. This expected delay is multiplied by the average number of removals per day to give a mean number of parts in the repair pipeline.[4] Assuming that the number of parts in resupply has a Poisson probability distribution, the standard deviation is the square root of the mean.[5]

---

[4]This computation is an application of Little's Theorem, or the "flow equation," frequently written as $L = \lambda W$. It says that for any system with objects flowing though it, assuming anything that goes in eventually comes out, the long-run average number in the system is equal to the flow rate times the average time objects spend in the system. This may be obvious, and apparently some authors think so, because Little's Theorem is sometimes invoked without any indication that it is being applied.

[5]In the Air Force's application, the standard deviation computed this way was multiplied by the square root of 3 to accommodate the observation that variances of pipeline contents are usually greater than the mean. This was so that the safety factor, i.e., the number of standard deviations, would have meaning. In our use of the fixed safety level model, we did not care about the value of the safety factor because we constrained problems by budget.

The main virtue of FSL is simplicity. Its shortcomings are that it does not take into account interactions between depot and base stocks nor does it consider cost. These shortcomings were remedied with the introduction of METRIC.

METRIC

The name METRIC stands for *Multi-Echelon Technique for Recoverable Item Control*. We previously mentioned that METRIC seeks to minimize the total expected backorders summed over parts and bases subject to a budget constraint in a requirements application or to constraints on available spare parts in a pure stock leveling application. METRIC takes the number of parts in resupply to base supply to be a Poisson random variable. Beyond what has already been said, there are three aspects to understanding how METRIC works: how the distribution of the number of parts in resupply is used to calculate expected backorders, how the distribution of numbers in resupply is calculated from the pipeline model depicted in Figure 3.1, and how marginal analysis is applied to obtain an efficient tradeoff function between total expected backorders and the costs of the spare parts.

Calculating Expected Backorders from the Distribution of Parts in Resupply

From the definition of a stock level as on-hand plus due-ins minus due-outs, we have the equation

$$S = OH + DI - DO.$$

In this equation DI is the number of parts in resupply and DO is the backorders. Rearranging, we have

$$DO = OH + DI - S.$$

The number of backorders, or DO, will be greater than zero if and only if OH is zero and the number in resupply, or DI, is greater than the stock level, S. In that case, the number of backorders is the amount by which the number of parts in resupply exceeds the stock level. Given the density function, $f(x)$, for the number in resupply, the expected backorders, which we now call $EBO(S)$ rather than DO, is

$$EBO(S) = \sum_{x>S}(x-S)f(x). \tag{1}$$

Distribution of the Number of Parts in Resupply

Since the distribution of the number of parts in resupply is taken to be Poisson, we need to calculate the mean, μ. According to Palm's Theorem this is the daily removal rate, λ, multiplied by the expected interval between the removal of a part and the appearance of its replacement in base supply. The expected interval is a weighted average of the mean time spent in the base repair pipeline and the mean time for a requisition to be filled from the depot. The weight is the NRTS rate. The time for a requisition to be filled from the depot always includes the order-and-ship time, but may or may not include the time for retrograde and depot repair, depending on whether there is stock in the depot when the part is requisitioned. Let us call the expected delay between the time a requisition is sent to the depot and the replacement part enters the order-and-ship pipeline the depot delay time, or DDT for short. So far, we have

$$\mu = \lambda \big[(1-r)BRT + r(OST + DDT) \big], \tag{2}$$

where r is the NRTS rate, BRT is the mean time for a part in the base repair pipeline, and OST is the mean order-and-ship time. What remains is the calculation of DDT.

If we designate the systemwide removal rate by Λ, the rate at which parts go into the retrograde plus depot repair pipelines is Λr, and the mean time spent in those pipelines is known. Palm's Theorem applies, so that the probability distribution of the number of parts in that portion of the network is Poisson with mean equal to the expected pipeline times multiplied by Λr. We care about the mean number of requisitions that are held up at the depot for the lack of stock. These are depot backorders, and they are calculated from the depot stock level and distribution of the number in the retrograde plus depot repair pipelines in exactly the same way as we described to compute base supply's expected backorders from the distribution of the number of parts in resupply to the base.

Now we have the mean number of requisitions delayed at the depot, but what we really want to know is DDT, the expected time that requisitions are delayed. The translation is done by Little's Theorem, which says the expected waiting time is the expected number waiting divided by the flow rate, Λr.

To summarize, the calculation of expected backorders for a part at a base goes like this:

- By Palm's Theorem, the probability distribution of parts in the retrograde plus depot repair pipeline is Poisson with mean equal to the product of the systemwide removal rate, the NRTS rate, and the sum of the mean retrograde and depot repair pipeline times.

- The expected number of requisitions delayed in the retrograde and depot repair pipelines for lack of serviceable parts in depot stock is given by equation (1), where f is the distribution obtained in the previous step and S is the depot stock level. Call this the depot *EBO*.

- By Little's Theorem, the expected delay in filling a requisition at the depot for lack of serviceable parts in stock, *DDT*, is the depot *EBO* divided by Λr.

- By Palm's Theorem, the probability distribution of the number of parts in resupply to base supply is Poisson whose mean is computed by equation (2).

- The expected backorders at the base for the part is given by equation (1), with f from the previous step and S being the base's stock level for the part.

Note the similarity between the first two and last two steps. In fact, METRIC can be extended to more echelons, with calculations beginning with the highest echelon and moving toward the bases in a recursive manner. We should also point out that there are recursive formulas that make the computations simpler than they seem from our description.[6]

Applying Marginal Analysis

The earlier discussion of optimization indicated that the marginal analysis involves searching over three dimensions (parts, bases, and depot stock levels), yet the problem needs to be decomposed into a series of one-dimensional searches to be tractable. In METRIC this is done by performing the marginal analysis with one part at a time, making allocations of the part to the depot and across the bases. Each single-part problem is two-dimensional, involving depot stock and base stocks. Further decomposition is achieved by making a series of allocations to bases for each value of depot stock over a useful range. The result from applying this procedure to a part is a list giving, for each possible value of total stock (depot stock plus all that has been allocated across the bases), the expected backorders and every base's stock level. The results from all parts are then merged, again using marginal analysis, to produce the efficient tradeoff function between total expected backorders and the costs of the parts.[7]

---

[6]Equation (1) should be regarded as a definition rather than a formula for computation. Fortunately, $EBO(S)$ can be computed recursively. $EBO(0)$ is the mean of f. For $S > 0$, $EBO(S + 1) = EBO(S) - 1 + F(S)$, where F is the CDF corresponding to f. The CDF is also easy to compute because the density function of the Poisson distribution also lends itself to a simple recursive calculation. If the mean is μ, $f(0) = \exp(-\mu)$ and $f(x + 1) = \mu f(x) / (x + 1)$.

[7]In general, expected backorders as a function of cost for a part has points of nonconvexity, which is a violation of the conditions stated in footnote 3. This would interfere with proper merging across parts. The solution is to adjust the expected backorder values of the nonconvex points so that con-

Depot Stock and "Flushout"

We previously mentioned the intuitively appealing idea that, in the absence of lateral supply, when parts are scarce it would be a good tactic to keep the few that are available in depot supply and wait to see which customers are going to need them. But if many parts are available, it would be better to distribute them to the customers. One can watch METRIC allocate a part and observe that it does behave in the manner described. The initial allocations, up to a point, are to the depot. Then one more allocation causes a complete rearrangement of the stocks, with a few retained at the depot and the rest distributed to the bases. This phenomenon is called *flushout*. Not so appealing, however, is that as the allocation process proceeds, depot stock will eventually build up again and flushout events will recur. Figure 3.2 shows graphically how depot stock goes up and down as additional stock is allocated. The data used for this example are taken from Sherbrooke (1992). In the example, there are five bases, all having the same characteristics. It is in this kind of symmetric situation that the recurring flushout phenomenon is most noticeable.

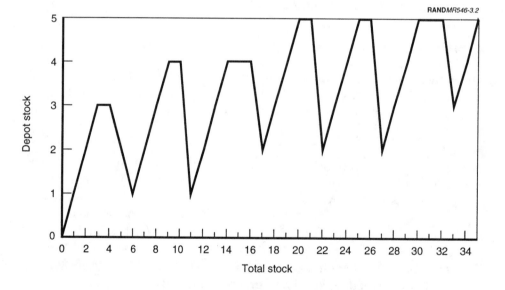

Figure 3.2—METRIC's Depot Stock as a Function of Total Stock

vex functions are obtained. All stock leveling and related processes that we know about have this problem.

FILL RATE

Fill rate is the probability that a part will be available in base supply when needed. In the formula $S = OH + DI - DO$, fill rate is the probability that OH is greater than zero. If $OH > 0$, then $DO = 0$ (there cannot be both stock on the shelf and backorders), and $OH = S - DI$. For OH to be positive, DI must be less than S. DI is the number in resupply, which is the random variable whose probability distribution METRIC uses to compute expected backorders. Rather than use equation (1), a fill rate model would calculate expected fill rate as $F(S - 1)$, where F is the cumulative distribution function of the number of parts in re-supply.

The previous paragraph was concerned with a single kind of part at one base, and we need to specify how to combine all those measures into an overall objective function. One way is to maximize the probability that a part is available wherever it may be required. Then the objective function should be the sum of all fill rates weighted by their respective removal rates.

VARI-METRIC

VARI-METRIC (Sherbrooke, 1986) is a refinement of METRIC to approximately correct for a faulty assumption in METRIC. Previously we stated that Palm's Theorem allowed us to claim that the distribution of parts in resupply to base supply was Poisson. But Palm's Theorem requires that the resupply times be independent random variables. This is not the case, however. If a requisition is placed on the depot at a time when the depot is stocked out, the requisition will be delayed, and there is a good chance that the same will happen to the next requisition for the part. Conversely, if there is stock on hand at the depot, it is likely that several requisitions in a row will be filled without delay. Because of this dependence, the variance of the number of parts in resupply to base supply is greater than the mean, and the distribution is not Poisson. The VARI-METRIC approximation[8] consists of calculating a variance, as well as a mean, for the number of parts in resupply and then assuming that the distribution is of the negative binomial form. Readers interested in the details can refer to Sherbrooke (1986) or to Sherbrooke (1992).

THE AIRCRAFT AVAILABILITY MODEL (AAM)

Although controlling expected backorders is an admirable goal, a model with an objective function more nearly related to a notion of aircraft availability is de-

---

[8]An exact solution is known (Simon, 1971) but is too computationally complicated for practical application.

sirable. The AAM (O'Malley, 1983) exploits METRIC to produce a measure of aircraft availability that can be interpreted as the probability that an airplane selected at random is missing none of its parts, assuming that parts shortages are randomly distributed among aircraft. For one base, the formula that relates this notion of availability to METRIC's expected backorders is

$$A = \prod_i \left(1 - \frac{EBO_i(S_i)}{Nq_i}\right)^{q_i}. \tag{3}$$

In the formula, $EBO_i(S_i)$ is the expected backorders for part i at the base; it is provided by a METRIC computation. N is the number of aircraft at the base, and q_i is the number of copies of part i that appear on an airplane. The crucial idea is that $EBO_i(S_i)/Nq_i$ is taken to be the probability that any type-i part selected at random in the fleet is missing. Then $(1 - EBO_i(S_i)/Nq_i)$ is the probability that a randomly selected part is not missing. The product taken over all parts in an airplane is the probability that an airplane selected at random is not missing any of its parts.

The AAM is of particular interest because it is the only procedure we considered that explicitly takes into account weapon system complexity.

As long as the problem involves only a single base (or multiple identical bases), it is possible to do marginal allocation of parts to the depot and base.[9] If, however, it is desired to allocate parts to more than one base, marginal allocation becomes intractable because all three dimensions (bases, parts, and depot stock) have to be juggled simultaneously; there is no way to break the problem down to a series of one-dimensional problems.

The Average Base Assumption

The Air Force's official version of the AAM, used in spares procurement requirements determination, avoids the difficulty just mentioned by constructing an "average base" for each weapon system. While arguably acceptable for that purpose, actual base differences should be accounted for in setting stock levels. Our approach is to eliminate the depot stock calculation from the optimization by taking depot stock levels computed outside the model as data. (In the spirit of consistency, we used an average base version of the AAM for this purpose.) Given a set of depot stock levels, it is possible to use marginal analysis to make a set of allocations of the various parts to each base in turn. Then the question is

---

[9]The objective function is converted to a sum as required by the condition stated in footnote 3 by taking logarithms.

how to mitigate among bases when combining the allocation lists for the individual bases. We have implemented two variants of the AAM for allocating stocks to heterogeneous bases.

Maximize Worldwide Availability

In this interpretation, an aircraft missing parts anywhere in the world counts the same as any other incomplete aircraft. The overall objective function then is the sum of the individual bases' availabilities weighted by the number of airplanes at the respective bases. When used in a requirements mode to allocate stocks subject to a budget constraint and the resulting set of stock levels are evaluated in a simulation, this method generally produces the best values of worldwide fully mission capable aircraft. As shown in later chapters, however, it also produces the widest base-to-base variation in availability. There are both weapon-system-complexity effects and base-size effects.

Bases with complex weapon systems (i.e., more parts) do worse than bases with simpler airplanes. This is because of the product form of a base's availability measure given by equation (3). A complex airplane has many parts, so there are many factors in the product, which dilutes the value of increasing the stock level for a part at the base during the marginal allocation. The base-size effect is that bases with more airplanes come out better than smaller bases. This is because the availabilities of large bases are weighted more heavily in the objective function and tend to attract a disproportionate number of assets.

Equalizing Availabilities

As an antidote to the effects just mentioned, we implemented a variant of the AAM that tries to allocate parts to bases in a way that brings up their respective availability measures in unison. As a requirements procedure, the problem can be stated as "Maximize the minimum base availability subject to a constraint on the total cost of parts." We call this version "Min-Base AAM." When subject to testing, it accomplishes the objective of producing nearly equal FMC rates across all bases regardless of size or the complexity of their airplanes.

THE AIR FORCE'S USE OF PIPELINE MODELS

Prior to 1975, the Air Force used a fixed safety level policy for requirements determination. In 1975, it implemented its variable safety level policy (VSL), which was an implementation of METRIC to address the requirements determination problem. For the first time in the requirements problem, the Air Force was able to make tradeoffs among items, giving up a few of the highest-cost items in favor of more low-cost items and achieving lower backorder rates for specific budgetary constraints. METRIC was a very popular innovation and was also adopted by the air forces of some allied nations as well as many commercial enterprises.

After several years of operation, VSL was replaced in 1989 by the Air Force's implementation of the Aircraft Availability Model, developed by the Logistics Management Institute. The AAM enabled the Air Force to account for weapon system complexity in its requirements determination process. An aircraft like the C-5, for example, which has many more LRUs than the typical aircraft, benefited from the AAM; moreover, the AAM quantified the availability-cost relationship for each weapon system and made it visible to decisionmakers for purposes of specifying aircraft availability targets. The AAM is in use to this day.

Chapter Four

APPLYING DRIVE TO STOCK LEVELING

Because DRIVE also employs marginal analysis, applying it to stock leveling is fairly straightforward and not much different from applying it to the generation of allocation lists. There are, however, some embellishments that can be made, both to DRIVE used in stock leveling and DRIVE as an execution system. This chapter gives an overview of DRIVE's algorithm and suggests how it can be made to attend to depot stocks and repair pipelines, both for stock leveling and for execution.

THE DRIVE ALGORITHM

DRIVE was originally conceived for application to short-horizon execution decisionmaking that takes into account current conditions. For this purpose, the steady-state assumptions made by models such as those described in Chapter Three are not appropriate. Instead, DRIVE looks out to a future point in time at the end of a relatively short planning horizon and asks, what can we do now to get to the best state at the end of the planning horizon? DRIVE's notion of availability is different from that of the AAM. In DRIVE, availability goals are specified for every kind of aircraft at every base. (To avoid verbiage, we will refer to a combination of aircraft and base simply as a base.) DRIVE's objective function is to repair and allocate parts to maximize the probability that all bases meet their availability goals at the end of the planning horizon. An important observation in the empirical work done in this body of research is that the optimal length of the planning horizon is equal to a part's weighted resupply time. We discuss this finding further in Chapter Seven.

DRIVE assumes that bases practice cannibalization so that holes (parts shortages) are consolidated in the fewest number of aircraft. Since the part at a base that is responsible for the most unavailable airplanes is the one that determines the base's availability, a base's availability goal can be extended to each part as an allowable number missing from aircraft. A base will meet its availability goal if the number missing is not more than the allowable number for any part.

Thus, the probability that a base meets its goal is the product of the probabilities that the individual parts meet their goals. The overall objective is the product of the base probabilities.

In dealing with the individual part-at-a-base probability, DRIVE needs an estimate of the probability distribution for the number of parts that are removed from airplanes during the planning horizon. This distribution is developed from knowledge of the part's failure rate, NRTS rate, and the base's anticipated flying program. We make an assumption about the variance, such as applying the Sherbrooke regression (Sherbrooke, 1984), and fit a negative binomial distribution to the data. A part will meet its goal if the number of removals during the horizon is no greater than the number of spare parts on hand at the start of the horizon less any existing holes, plus any parts allocated to the base, plus the allowable missing.

DRIVE allocates parts, one at a time, to bases using a marginal analysis procedure. For marginal analysis to be correct, the objective function has to be a sum, whereas DRIVE's, like the AAM's, is a product. As in the AAM, this is easily remedied by taking logarithms. The denominator of the sort value should be a measure of the consumption of whatever resource is most constraining. For the purpose of determining execution priorities, we recommended using standard repair hours. This also applies to DRIVE's application to stock leveling. We find it expedient, as in METRIC, to perform allocations for one part at a time and merge the results afterward using the sort values accompanying each allocation step.

WHY DRIVE?

There have been some criticisms of DRIVE: the objective of meeting availability goals is binary; values of its overall objective function are invisibly small; it is unaware of pipelines; it tends to make its first allocations to the smaller bases; and it assumes cannibalization. On the other hand, DRIVE has a number of advantages in the applications for which it was originally intended. DRIVE was devised to set priorities for depot repair and allocation of parts, and its algorithm is naturally compatible with that purpose. Its objective function is related to aircraft availability, it has no difficulty dealing with heterogeneous bases, and it allows differential treatment of bases through goal setting. Because DRIVE is not based on long-run, steady-state probabilities, it is compatible with short-term scenarios and offers a natural way to integrate the allocation of primary operating stock (POS) and readiness spares package (RSP) assets. Most important to its original application, DRIVE is highly sensitive to the current asset position. The form of its objective function allows DRIVE to treat two levels of indenture in a way that is more realistic than the approaches taken by pipeline models. We will return to this point at the end of the chapter.

DRIVE FOR STOCK LEVELING

To employ DRIVE as a stock leveling procedure, we can start with the assumption that bases have neither stock on hand nor holes, and let DRIVE allocate parts up to a stopping point. In the stock leveling application, DRIVE would be programmed to stop when it reached the stopping point or until it ran out of assets, whichever occurred first. The standard repair hours would be used in the denominators of the sort values, and the merged list of parts would be cut off where the total cost of parts equaled the specified budget.

Using DRIVE in this way as an aid in calculating requirements is problematical if one wishes to make judgments from an availability-cost tradeoff function. The reason is that the value of DRIVE's objective function, being the product of a large number of probabilities, is not likely to be very meaningful.

Implementing DRIVE as a Stock Leveling System

Applying DRIVE to real-world stock leveling is straightforward. The vehicle of choice is Desktop DRIVE. The stock leveling problem should be constrained to a fairly homogeneous set of items repaired in one or a few shops. The F-16 avionics LRUs and SRUs repaired at Ogden are a good example of such a set of items. We envision releveling occurring quarterly or whenever events occur that significantly change the aircraft availability goals, force beddown, aircraft configuration, flying hour program, repair or transportation times, NRTS rates, or other factors that affect item-base pipelines. In determining quarterly repair requirements for LRUs and SRUs, DRIVE produces a globally optimized, sequenced list of repair actions. The list reflects carcass constraints and is made to be much longer than it needs to be.

Decisionmaking about quarterly repair requirements always involves the application of constraints, usually budgetary or repair capacity constraints. The more active of those constraints determines the actual length of the list of items that will be repaired. The globally optimized character of the sequenced list enables one to draw a line anywhere on the list, and for that total budget or repair capacity, the list above the line will approximately maximize the probability that all bases will meet their specified aircraft availability goals. Conversely, for that level of performance, the list above the line represents a least-cost repair mix.

In deciding where to draw the line so that it is as far down the list as possible but still satisfies the constraints he faces, the decisionmaker implicitly determines the end-of-quarter asset position that translates directly to the desired mix of stock levels. That mix of levels is approximately optimal for both LRUs and SRUs, given the constraints, and also satisfies carcass constraints, i.e., it will not allocate more stock levels of an item than there are assets of that item in the inventory system.

Setting stock levels with Desktop DRIVE requires very little further development. Running DRIVE in its quarterly repair requirements mode enables one to determine stock levels implicitly, and Ogden has been successfully determining quarterly repair requirements for F-16 avionics LRUs and SRUs with DRIVE for several years. Its extension to central stock leveling is perfectly natural.

Reluctant DRIVE: Making DRIVE Attend to Depot Stock

The motivation for allocating stock levels to the depot has been mentioned. But DRIVE as we have described it does not hold back any parts from the bases. An ideal determination of the proper balance between base and depot stocks ought to take into account the relative delays in having parts readily available at bases versus the longer time necessary to ship a part from the depot to a base after the need arises, as do the METRIC-based models in Chapter Three. But there is no way (that we could think of) to incorporate such time-delay considerations into DRIVE's underlying view of the world. Lacking an ideal approach, we devised the following, which we call *Reluctant DRIVE*.

At any stage in the marginal allocation process for a part, DRIVE computes the probability for each base that removals of the part will not cause the base to miss meeting its availability goal. If we multiply together all the bases' probabilities, the product can be interpreted as being the probability that none of the bases will require a part from the depot during the horizon to meet its availability goal. Assume that the number of parts that will be needed for all bases to meet their goals has a Poisson probability distribution. The product of probabilities just described is the probability of the zero point of the distribution. If we designate that probability as P_0, then $P_0 = e^{-\mu}$, where μ is the mean of the Poisson distribution,[1] and $\mu = -\ln P_0$. Our somewhat heuristic approach is to calculate sort values for depot stock based on this distribution. After each normal allocation of a part to the depot, compute the resulting μ and P_0. With sort values based on the resulting Poisson distribution, allocate stock to the depot

---

[1] Recall that the density function of the Poisson distribution is given by $P(x) = e^{-\mu}\mu^x/x!$, $x = 0, 1, 2, \ldots$, and 0 elsewhere.

until a sort value is reached that is at least as small as the sort value observed at the last allocation to a base.

We call this approach Reluctant DRIVE after the work of Bruce Miller (1968), who invented a scheme called *Real Time METRIC* that does away with stock levels entirely. Miller's idea was to compute bases' *needs* at the occurrence of every significant change of state. A base's need is defined as the expected number of backorders at the end of a depot-to-base shipping time. The need is compared to a *depot reluctance* function that is a decreasing function of stock on hand. By comparing a base's need with the depot's reluctance, a decision is made as to whether or not to send a part to the base.

Accounting for Base Repair Pipelines

DRIVE, in its original configuration, did not supply LRUs to protect base repair pipelines. DRIVE, being conceived as a system for supplying parts from the depot, only sees demands filtered by NRTS rates. In fact, DRIVE has a built-in bias against protecting base repair pipelines on the theory that the depot should not be sending out LRUs when bases have LRUs that should be coming out of their own shops soon, particularly if they prove to be "bench check serviceable."[2] Whether or not this judgment was correct, DRIVE used for stock leveling should attend to supplying spares to cover parts in base repair. This is particularly true for LRUs that have high removal rates coupled with low NRTS rates.

A fairly obvious adjustment is to augment DRIVE's estimate of the expected number of demands that is used to calculate the probability distributions upon which the allocations are based. Currently DRIVE calculates the mean demand as a removal rate times the NRTS rate times the planning horizon length. The modification that worked well in our simulations consisted of adding in the removal rate times one minus the NRTS rate times an average base repair time. As we discuss in Chapter Seven, the empirical evaluations carried out in this body of work suggest a weighted resupply time as the most appropriate planning horizon length.

RELUCTANT DRIVE FOR EXECUTION

As already pointed out, DRIVE allocates all available serviceable parts to bases; however, it may sometimes pay to retain parts at the depot, presumably for the same reason that we have outlined for having depot stocks when parts are in

---

[2]DRIVE does, however, have elaborate mechanisms to supply bases with spare SRUs for the bases to use in their repair operations. Much of DRIVE's complexity derives from the inclusion of SRUs.

short supply.   The same basic idea underlying Reluctant DRIVE for stock leveling can be applied to execution DRIVE.

Although the Ogden Prototype of DRIVE was run once every two weeks, we expect that DRIVE will be run much more frequently with the advent of Desktop DRIVE, at least for the purpose of allocating serviceable parts. In a near-real-time use of DRIVE, there are two events that call for a decision as to whether to keep or send: receipt of a requisition and the emergence of a serviceable LRU from repair.

When a requisition is received, it is possible to perform the same calculation to obtain a value for μ that was described previously. Knowing the number of LRUs on hand at the depot, calculate a sort value associated with adding another LRU to the depot's stock. This sort value can be compared with the corresponding sort value for the base making the requisition, and a decision made based on which sort value is higher. We recommend one refinement: When computing P_0, do not include in the product of bases' probabilities the probability associated with the base making the requisition. The effect of this is to lower the depot's sort value and make it more likely that the LRU will be sent. This adjustment was suggested by our experience with simulation. Without the adjustment, at least in cases involving small numbers of bases, it appeared that the depot won the contest more often than it should have.

The other occasion requiring a keep-or-send decision is when the repair of an LRU has been completed. DRIVE knows to what base it wants to send the LRU, and there is a corresponding sort value. If keeping the part would make the depot's stock on hand greater than the depot's stock level, the part should be sent to the base. Also, if the base needs the part to meet its availability goal, the part should be sent. Otherwise, the same kind of comparison as is made upon the receipt of a requisition should be done.

A further refinement is inspired by the flushout phenomenon. It is conceivable that when a part is sent to a base in conjunction with a repair completion event, the P_0 value that is the basis of the reluctance computation might improve enough that even more parts should be sent to bases. If a part is sent to a base, then repeat the comparison with an updated value for P_0, and continue this way until either a decision is made not to send a part or the depot's inventory is depleted.

We have tried all of the ideas above in our Dyna-METRIC simulations, but have not found compelling evidence that withholding parts at the depot improves performance when DRIVE is being used in execution, i.e., for repair prioritization and asset allocation. As suggested by results presented in later chapters, with DRIVE used to prioritize repair and allocate assets, there is little or nothing to be gained by withholding parts from the bases. Without DRIVE in execution, keeping some serviceable parts at the depot may improve performance by act-ing as a buffer.

TWO VARIATIONS OF DRIVE

During the course of this research we implemented two variations of DRIVE.

VARI-METRIC DRIVE

As the name suggests, VARI-METRIC DRIVE is a marriage of VARI-METRIC and DRIVE. The idea is to allocate parts using DRIVE's marginal analysis scheme, but instead of employing DRIVE's probability distributions for part removals during a planning horizon, use VARI-METRIC's distributions of backorders. The motivation was that since DRIVE is oblivious to pipeline delays, it can be made aware by using probability distributions derived from considerations of those delays. Another way of viewing VARI-METRIC DRIVE is that it is VARI-METRIC, but instead of using total worldwide expected backorders as the ob-jective function, it seeks to optimize against DRIVE's goal of maximizing the probability of all bases meeting their availability goals, but in the steady state rather than at the end of a finite horizon.

Min-Base DRIVE

As will be seen in later chapters, simulation results using stock levels calculated by DRIVE display base size and weapon system complexity effects similar to those observed from stock levels set by METRIC and Worldwide AAM. Min-Base DRIVE was invented as a possible remedy, as the Min-Base version of the AAM was. Rather than allocate LRUs one at a time across bases and then merge those results as DRIVE normally does, the procedure is reversed. Like Min-Base AAM, Min-Base DRIVE allocates all LRUs to one base at a time. When that is done, every base has a sequenced list of LRUs to be allocated along with the corresponding probabilities of the base meeting its availability goal. Then those results are merged, but the criterion in building up the solution is to always choose the base with the least overall probability of meeting its goal.

CONSIDERATION OF SRUs

Although we believe that DRIVE's way of dealing with SRUs is superior to the methods found in pipeline models, SRUs were not included in this research. To have done so would have added a great amount of complexity, and we judged that it was important to understand first-order effects by working with only one level of indenture before examining more complicated cases.

Multi-Echelon Extensions of Pipeline Models

Pipeline models make two complementary assumptions. The first is that the repair of every LRU requires exactly one SRU, regardless of how many SRUs are contained in the LRU. In modeling, the demand for SRUs is conditional on the demand for LRUs, and a probability distribution governing the choice of which SRU is required for any LRU repair is given as data. The complementary assumption, employed in calculating the distribution of numbers of LRUs in resupply, is that any SRU needed for the repair of its parent LRU will, if not in stock, add to the LRU's pipeline time. With these assumptions, pipeline models are capable of accommodating an arbitrary number of levels of indenture. The earliest multi-echelon extension of pipeline models was "Mod-METRIC" (Muckstadt, 1973), and more recently, VARI-METRIC.

SRUs in DRIVE

DRIVE considers SRUs from two perspectives: to support depot repair of LRUs and to supply stocks of spare SRUs to bases (Miller and Abell, 1992). For LRUs repaired at the depot, DRIVE assumes that the demand for SRUs is derived from LRUs, but there is no constraint on how many SRUs an LRU may need. DRIVE also prioritizes the repair and allocation of SRUs for bases that have LRU repair capability. For that purpose, demands for SRUs at bases are assumed to be primary events (i.e., not conditional on LRU removals), and DRIVE calculates the implication of SRU shortages to LRU availability using a cannibalization assumption.

There seems to be no apparent reason why DRIVE's approach to SRUs cannot be adapted for allocating SRU stock levels as well as for LRUs.

Chapter Five

THE EVALUATIONS: SCENARIO, DESIGN, RESULTS, AND OBSERVATIONS

In this chapter, we discuss the analytic design with which we evaluated the alternative stock leveling approaches, the results of the evaluations, and some observations we made during the course of the analysis.

SCENARIO AND ANALYTIC DESIGN

Although we used several scenarios in these evaluations, our principal scenario and the one underlying the results presented throughout this chapter is described here. It comprises two weapon systems, six bases, and 135 LRUs, 27 of which are common to both weapon systems. Weapon system 1 is the less complex one; it has 54 LRUs. Thus, half the LRUs in the smaller aircraft are shared by the more complex aircraft. The larger aircraft has 108 LRUs. Weapon system 1, the simpler one, is at bases 1, 3, and 5, and weapon system 2, the more complex one, is at bases 2, 4, and 6. For each weapon system, there is one base with 18 primary authorized aircraft (PAA), one with 36, and one with 72. The same is true for the more complex aircraft. Thus, there are two 18-PAA, two 36-PAA, and two 72-PAA bases. The force beddown is shown in Figure 5.1.

RAND*MR546-5.1*

Base	1	2	3	4	5	6
Weapon system	1	2	1	2	1	2
PAA	18	18	36	36	72	72

Figure 5.1—Force Beddown in the Analytic Scenario

Variations of this scenario that received less comprehensive analysis included one with 24 bases, one with fewer LRUs, and one with actual data on the B-1B weapon system.[1]

It is important to note that we excluded SRUs from these evaluations. Each aircraft comprises some multiple of a basic set of 27 LRUs. In each set of LRUs there is exactly one LRU for each unique combination of OIM (organizational and intermediate maintenance) demand rate, NRTS (not repairable this station) rate, and cost. The possible values of each of these item characteristics were as follows: OIM demand rate was either 0.1, 0.2, or 0.4; NRTS rate was either 0.1, 0.5, or 0.9; and cost was either 1, 2, or 4 units. Thus, there are 3 times 3 times 3 equals 27 combinations of item characteristics.

We decided to create the LRUs for most of the evaluations because it gave us complete control over weapon system complexity and item characteristics. It turned out to yield some information that might otherwise have gone unnoticed, most notably the need to add the base repair pipeline to the expected demands in DRIVE's planning horizon.

The retrograde time was specified to be 20 days; the on-stand time at the depot, exclusive of queueing, 1 day; the order-and-ship time 2 days; and the base repair time 5 days. In those cases where we specified lateral supply in the evaluation, the lateral resupply time was 2 days, the same as the order-and-ship time. All aircraft were assumed to fly 30 hours per month.

We used Poisson demands for most cases, but also tried several others. In some evaluations, we specified VTMRs as high as 5.0.

We used Dyna-METRIC Version 6 for the evaluations, and modified it to include DRIVE in execution (Isaacson and Boren, 1993). Any time Dyna-METRIC needed to repair an asset or allocate a serviceable, it called on DRIVE to make the decision. Thus, DRIVE effectively operated in real time.

We specified the number of test stands at the depot repair facility such that the utilization rate was approximately 0.9.

RESULTS

Figure 5.2 shows METRIC's performance in terms of aircraft availability observed at each of the six bases. The aircraft availability rates shown are the average observed values of 600 observations, 10 replications of 600-day runs, each of which yielded 20 observations 30 days apart. In this design, auto-

---

[1]The B-1B data were kindly provided by Mr. Bob McCormick, Headquarters, AFMC/XPSA.

RAND*MR546-5.2*

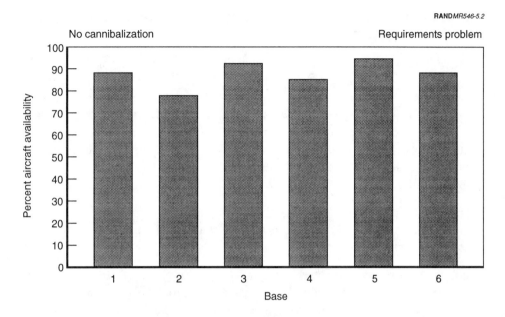

Figure 5.2—METRIC's Performance by Base and Weapon System

correlation is virtually eliminated. Thus, the error variance is quite small. The standard deviation of the worldwide aircraft availability associated with the system performance portrayed in Figure 5.2, for example, is about 0.52 percent.

The stock levels being evaluated throughout the discussion that follows, unless otherwise noted, are the results of solutions to the requirements problem, not the pure stock leveling problem. They assume no cannibalization or perfect cannibalization, as shown above each graph, and no lateral supply. If one observes the performance at bases 1, 3, and 5, one can see the effect of base size on aircraft availability for weapon system 1, the less complex aircraft. The same is true of bases 2, 4, and 6 for the more complex aircraft. If one compares base 1 with base 2, base 3 with base 4, or base 5 with base 6, one can see the effect of weapon system complexity, i.e., we are doubling the number of LRUs in an aircraft within these base pairs. As we will show presently, this mix of aircraft availabilities is typical of all the approaches that focus on optimizing a global measure of performance. As in all of the evaluations that follow, unless otherwise stated, DRIVE is used in execution in Dyna-METRIC.

Global Optimization May Yield Unacceptable Differences Among Bases and Weapon Systems

Figure 5.2 shows the aircraft availability delivered at each of the six bases in the scenario by the stock levels determined by METRIC. The availability rates at individual bases in this case range from 77.1 to 94.5 percent, a difference of over 17 percent of possessed aircraft. While this may be an "optimal" mix against a global measure of performance, as a practical matter it may not be a satisfactory solution. Consider it from the point of view of the unit commander at base 2. The central system is allocating resources in a way that he may think of as penalizing him.

Even if all units consolidate parts shortages perfectly, i.e., in the case of full cannibalization, the availability rates at bases 2 and 5 still differ by about 5 percent of possessed aircraft.

The important point illustrated in Figure 5.2 is that, although it may be desirable to allow this heterogeneity in performance among bases or weapon systems, the goal-setter should know exactly what his goals imply, base by base and weapon system by weapon system, and address these performance differences explicitly.

As Figure 5.3 shows, the version of the Aircraft Availability Model that maximizes worldwide availability (AAM WW) performs quite similarly to METRIC. The heterogeneity among bases is somewhat worse, but the mix of observed availabilities is essentially the same. Again, these evaluations assumed no cannibalization. In Figure 5.3, as in all of the comparisons of results that follow, the same budgetary constraint was used for each method.

The third set of bars in Figure 5.4 represents DRIVE's performance against the same measure with the same assumption of no cannibalization. Note the similarity between DRIVE's performance and METRIC's.

Recall that the standard deviation of METRIC's worldwide performance is 0.52 percent. The standard deviation of DRIVE's worldwide performance is about 0.72 percent. The random number streams used in both evaluations were the same; therefore, the standard deviation of the difference in the worldwide performance of the two approaches is only 0.41 percent. Thus, it's probably fair to say that performance differences visible in the graphs discussed in this and the following two chapters are generally statistically significant. A 1 percent difference is roughly two and a half standard deviations.

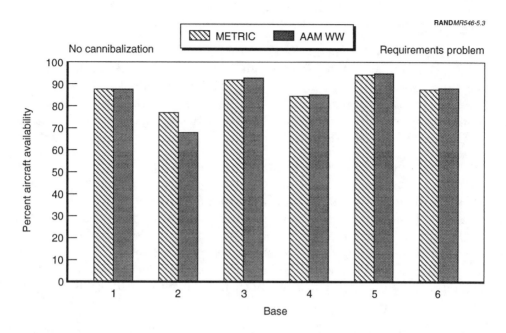

Figure 5.3—The AAM's Performance Is Similar to METRIC's

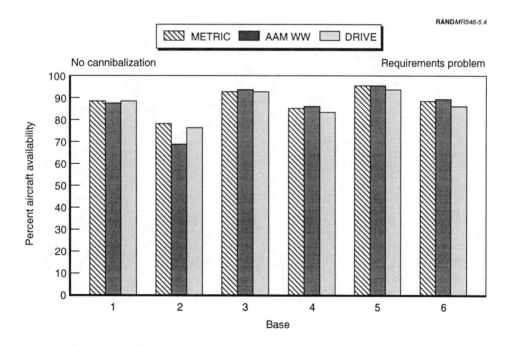

Figure 5.4—DRIVE's Performance Is Similar to Both

Optimization Methods Dominate a Fixed Safety Level Approach

In Figure 5.5, we add the performance of a fixed safety level policy to compare it with the performance of these three optimization models. The performance of the stock levels determined by the fixed safety level method is dominated at every single base by every other approach. In terms of worldwide aircraft availability, the fixed safety level policy delivers over 10 percent less availability (as a percentage of possessed aircraft) than the average of the other three methods.

SBSS and negotiated levels are much the same in concept as a fixed safety level approach. The levels are disconnected from the worldwide asset position. These methods lack a system view; therefore, the levels they compute aren't connected to anything, not even other stock levels at the same base, and certainly not to an aircraft availability goal. Thus, there is no account taken of unit costs, no tradeoff among items, bases, or weapon systems. The fixed safety level approach is similar to the SBSS and the use of special or negotiated levels in all of these characteristics. None of them is nearly as cost-effective as any one of the optimization approaches.

There is an important lesson in Figure 5.5: Don't use SBSS levels when it is possible to use an optimization model.

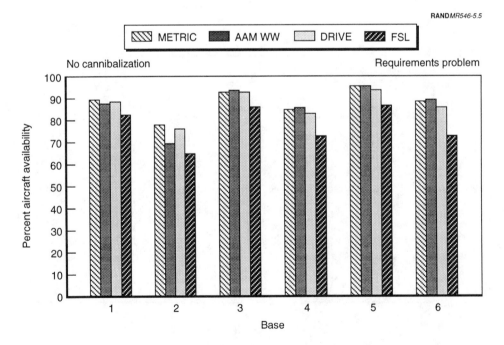

Figure 5.5—All Three Optimization Models Outperform an FSL Method

Since D028 is really an implementation of METRIC, it is clearly a superior approach to any in the fixed safety level family, including the SBSS. D028 may have data problems or systemic problems of which we are unaware, but setting such considerations aside, there is no doubt in our minds that, at least in principle, the approach taken in D028 is clearly superior to the SBSS in cost-effectiveness.

Simple Examples of Approaches to Equalize Performance Among Bases

There are several sensible approaches to dealing with the problem of unacceptable heterogeneity in performance among bases and weapon systems. The approaches we examine here are adaptations of the AAM and DRIVE to the problem of equalizing performance among the bases. They are not completely satisfying either, of course, since one might not want *equal* performance but, rather, differential performance among bases according to mission urgency, deployment sequencing, or other military considerations. The point is that equalizing performance is only one approach to the problem implicit in Figure 5.2, and we intend the discussion that follows only to be illustrative of what might be done to resolve it.

In Figure 5.6 we compare the performance of two representations of the Aircraft Availability Model, one that maximizes worldwide availability and one that operates with the constraint that it must always allocate the marginal stock level to the base with the lowest aircraft availability. In that way, the optimization procedure is forced to bring all the bases up to a specified availability goal together. As one can readily see here, it achieves that goal admirably well. While the difference in performance between the highest and lowest availabilities achieved by the AAM's worldwide optimization is 26.7 percent of possessed aircraft, the constrained procedure reduces that difference to less than 3 percent.

This particular approach is intended to achieve equal performance at all bases. We emphasize that it is only one of several possible approaches to constraining an optimization model. For example, one might wish to specify differential goals among bases and constrain the optimization algorithm to allocate the marginal stock level to the base with the aircraft availability that is the lowest *proportion* of its goal, thus bringing the bases up together to a differential mix of goals. There are other intuitively appealing approaches that might be more attractive than a global optimization. They should be explored jointly by policymakers and model developers.

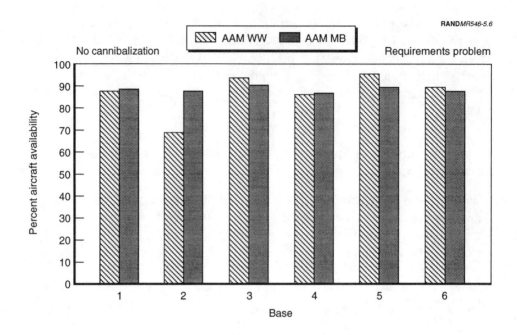

Figure 5.6—The "Minimum Base" Version of the AAM Compared with the AAM

As we mentioned earlier, we also developed an enhancement to DRIVE that attempts to equalize the probabilities of achieving the specified aircraft availability goals at all bases under an assumption of full cannibalization. The "minimum base" version of DRIVE takes that approach; however, note that equalizing the probabilities is not equivalent to equalizing the observed aircraft availabilities without cannibalization, as Figure 5.7 shows. This approach successfully eliminates the weapon-system effect, but the base-size effect is still there.

As Figure 5.8 shows, the constrained optimization procedure in the minimum base version of DRIVE (DRIVE MB) that tries to equalize the probabilities of achieving the availability goals at all the bases does that quite well in contrast to the unconstrained DRIVE. The probability of meeting a specified aircraft availability goal is a performance measure that is more consistent with DRIVE's objective function. Observed aircraft availability, although the appropriate measure of system performance as a practical matter, is slightly removed from DRIVE's central focus on the probability that all bases meet their specified availability goals. In this sense, as well as in the very small numerical values of DRIVE's objective function in most real-world applications, the objective function is somewhat troublesome.

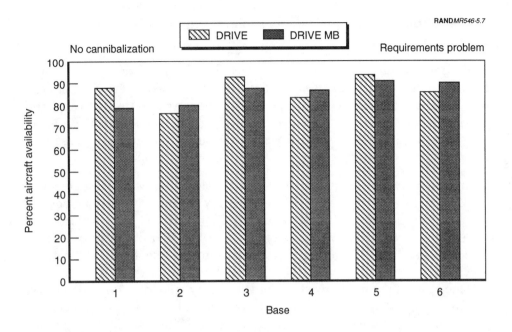

Figure 5.7—DRIVE Compared with Its Minimum Base Version

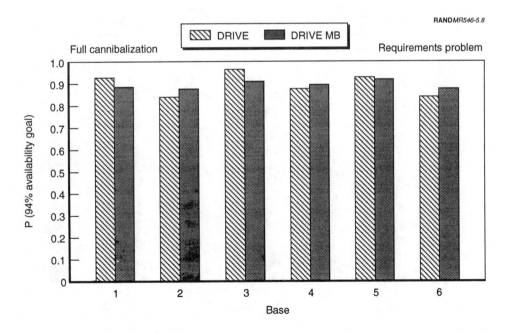

Figure 5.8—The Same Comparison Using Probabilities

The Solution to the Requirements Problem Dominates System Performance

As we pointed out in Chapter One, the actual problem solved by the central stock leveling system is a hybrid of what we have defined as the requirements problem and the pure stock leveling problem. What we show in Figures 5.9 and 5.10 is that the solution to the pure stock leveling problem has much less effect than that of the requirements problem because the solution to the requirements problem determines the richness of stock in the inventory system.

In implementation, the central stock leveling algorithm would allocate stock levels up to the number of assets in the inventory system or the number beyond which little contribution is made to system performance, whichever is less. For some items, it would determine the richness of assets in the system, and for others it would not. The results that follow point out that, for those assets for which the central stock leveling algorithm only solves the pure stock leveling problem, the choice of approach is not very important. This does not suggest that the choice of approach to the real-world stock leveling problem is unimportant because it solves both the requirements and pure stock leveling problems.

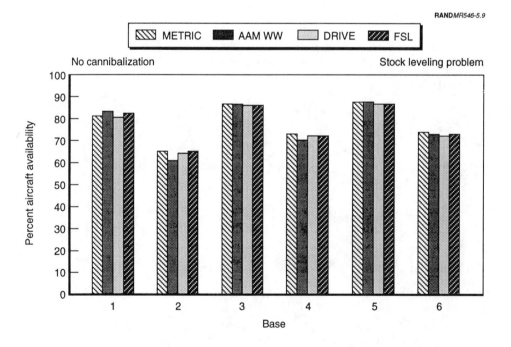

Figure 5.9—Stock Leveling Performance with Fixed Safety Level Requirements

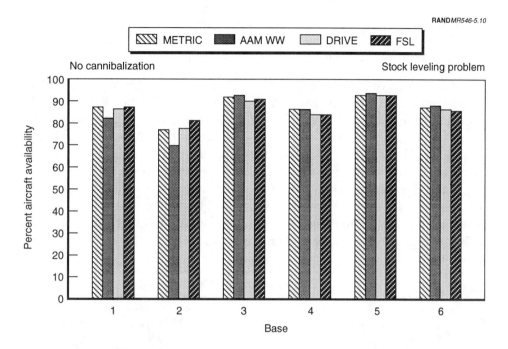

Figure 5.10—Stock Leveling Performance with AAM AB Requirements

Figures 5.9 and 5.10 underscore the important lesson that the solution to the requirements problem dominates the determination of system performance. In Figure 5.9, we portray the performance of METRIC, the AAM, DRIVE, and a fixed safety level approach in the pure stock leveling problem after the number of assets of each type in the inventory system is first determined by the fixed safety level calculation. The choice of stock leveling method matters little. This observation is of fundamental importance.

Figure 5.10 contrasts the performance of alternative approaches in the case where the version of the Aircraft Availability Model used in D041 (AAM AB) is used to determine requirements. The mix of assets in the inventory system is quite different in this case than in the case portrayed in Figure 5.9. Note the significant improvement in all of the pure stock leveling approaches when the AAM AB is used to determine the assets available. In this case, METRIC, for example, achieves availabilities of about 76 to 92 percent and a worldwide availability of about 88 percent. In the case shown in Figure 5.9, where the mix

of assets was computed by the fixed safety level method, METRIC achieved availabilities ranging from about 64 to 87 percent and a worldwide availability of about 79 percent, 9 percent less than with AAM AB asset levels. As one can readily see, the fixed safety level method doesn't do that much worse than

METRIC or the other optimization approaches in the pure stock leveling problem. Thus, it is clear that the vast majority of the leverage one has over system performance derives from the requirements solution.

Figure 5.11 portrays the performance of the stock levels determined by DRIVE in the requirements problem (in which it determined the mix of assets in the system as well as the stock levels) and in the pure stock leveling problem where the mix of assets was determined by the fixed safety level approach. The difference in global performance in these two cases is over 10 percent of possessed aircraft, a dramatic reinforcement of two earlier observations: (1) don't use a fixed safety level approach in lieu of an optimization method, and (2) most of the leverage over system performance lies in the solution to the requirements problem. It is the requirements solution that determines the richness of stock in the system, thereby gaining that leverage.

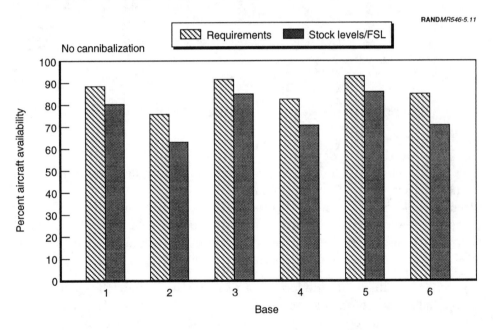

Figure 5.11—DRIVE's Performance in Both Problems

Chapter Six

THE RELATIONSHIP BETWEEN DEPOT STOCK AND DRIVE IN EXECUTION

Recall that the order-and-ship time in the scenario used in the discussion so far is only two days. In this particular scenario, METRIC allocates about 46 percent of the total stock levels to the depot. Yet when we constrained METRIC to have no depot stock (NDS), it did almost as well. The reason for this is the important fact that DRIVE was allocating assets and prioritizing repairs in Dyna-METRIC. In a sense, then, it is DRIVE in execution, coupled with higher stock levels at the bases, that enables METRIC to achieve such good performance without depot stock. In this chapter, we explore the important question of whether the logistics system can operate as effectively without depot stock as it can with depot stock and DRIVE in execution.

As Figure 6.1 shows, stock levels determined by Reluctant DRIVE and DRIVE achieve nearly the same levels of performance as METRIC's stock levels when no cannibalization is assumed, and virtually identical performance in the presence of full cannibalization.

Figure 6.2 delivers an important message about using DRIVE in the requirements problem. The sets of bars denoted "METRIC NDE" and "DRIVE NDE" portray METRIC's and DRIVE's performance in the requirements problem evaluated without DRIVE in execution in Dyna-METRIC ("NDE" signifies "no DRIVE in execution"). Note that the performance of the stock levels determined by DRIVE is considerably diminished without DRIVE in execution, but that METRIC's performance, although slightly diminished, holds up fairly well without DRIVE in execution.

The reason for this is that DRIVE allocates no stock levels to the depot, while METRIC allocates about 46 percent of the total stock levels in the system to the depot. Thus, base-level backorders occur less often with DRIVE's richer base stock levels, but without a role in execution, DRIVE is unable to prioritize the repair and allocation of assets at the depot. Since there is no depot stock, the backorder has to wait its turn, so to speak.

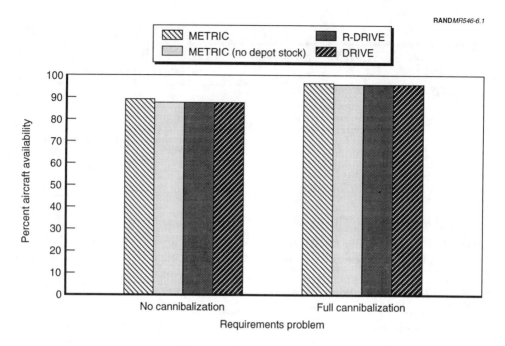

Figure 6.1—The Effects of Depot Stock Are Minimal with DRIVE in Execution

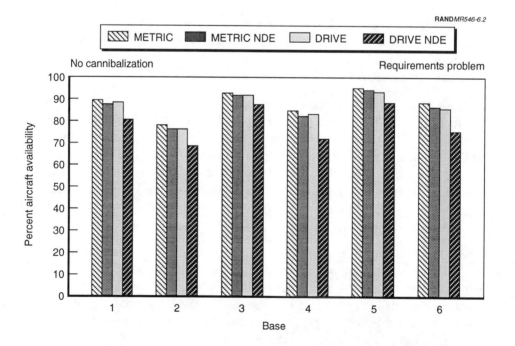

Figure 6.2—System Performance With and Without DRIVE in Execution

In METRIC's case, although base-level backorders are more frequent, they are filled more often by serviceables on the shelf at the depot. METRIC's depot stock levels make its performance more robust in the face of first-come-first-serve disciplines in repair and asset allocation.

This observation is verified in the next two figures, which portray the results of evaluations of METRIC with no depot stock (METRIC NDS) with and without DRIVE in execution, and contrasts its performance levels with those of DRIVE. Figure 6.3 assumes no cannibalization and Figure 6.4 assumes full cannibalization.

The overall effect of richer depot stock levels is to make base stock levels more lean. But with DRIVE in execution, it is important from the standpoint of performance that base stock levels are sufficiently rich that DRIVE's recommended asset allocations are not inhibited by lack of due-ins. DRIVE is able to enhance the contribution of depot repair to system performance very significantly. When all the stock levels are allocated to the bases, however, as DRIVE or METRIC NDS does, system performance becomes much more sensitive to depot responsiveness, which depends heavily on having DRIVE in execution. The full cannibalization case is shown in Figure 6.4.

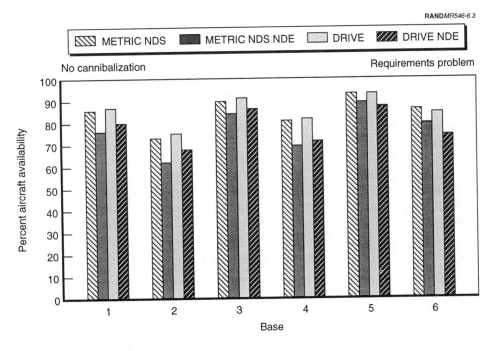

Figure 6.3—Without Depot Stock, METRIC's Performance Also Suffers Without DRIVE in Execution

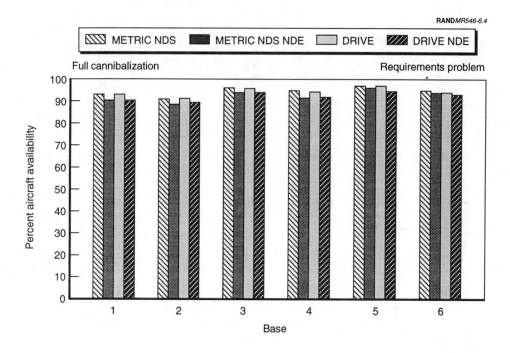

Figure 6.4—Full Cannibalization Helps Considerably

Our conclusion is that DRIVE should not be used to allocate stock levels unless it is also used in execution. A related question that is more difficult to answer is whether DRIVE should be used for stock leveling at all, since it allocates all the stock levels to the bases. Our evaluations suggest that DRIVE, properly supported and applied, is sufficiently powerful as a planning and execution decision support system as to obviate the need for depot stock, thus offering the possibility of dramatically reducing the costs associated with storing, maintaining, and administering it.

Based on past evaluations of DRIVE and our participation in its field demonstration, we have concluded that the importance of DRIVE's contributions to system performance can be ranked: (1) quarterly repair requirements determination, (2) repair prioritization, (3) asset allocation, and (4) stock leveling. As we pointed out earlier, the real-world stock leveling problem is, in fact, a hybrid of the requirements problem, as defined here, and the pure stock leveling problem. Using DRIVE to set stock levels will solve the problem of inconsistencies between depot allocations and base due-ins, but has the additional attraction of enhanced system performance when base stock levels are not inhibiting its allocations of assets from the depot, which is more likely to occur when stock levels are being determined by an approach that diminishes base stock levels in favor of depot stock levels. In other words, the richer stock levels at the bases that derive from using DRIVE to determine them tend to free DRIVE in execution from the constraints it would face if another stock leveling approach were used that allocated stock levels to the depot at the expense of base levels.

Chapter Seven

SETTING AVAILABILITY GOALS AND PLANNING HORIZONS IN DRIVE

Here we examine DRIVE's performance in the requirements problem when the availability goals are specified to be less than 100 percent.

AVAILABILITY GOALS LESS THAN 100 PERCENT

In Figures 7.1 and 7.2, we show some evaluative results in the case where the availability goals were specified to be less than 100 percent at each of the six bases. In the first case we will discuss here, we specified the goal to be 94 percent at every base, because with 94 percent goals, one, two, and four aircraft are allowed to be unavailable at the 18-, 36-, and 72-PAA bases, respectively, and the goals can still be met. It is the highest goal less than 100 percent that allows any aircraft to be down at the smallest base and still meet the goals.

The two leftmost bars shown for each base in Figure 7.1 represent the performance of DRIVE and its minimum base version in the requirements problem under an assumption of no cannibalization with goals of 100 percent availability. The two rightmost bars at each base show their performance when 94 percent aircraft availability goals are specified at each base. In the absence of cannibalization, DRIVE's allocation of stock levels with these lower goals heavily favors the smaller bases at the expense of the larger ones. The stockage postures underlying this performance with reduced goals are very different from those associated with 100 percent goals, incorporating a shift in the allocation of stock levels from the larger bases to the smaller ones and a corresponding shift in performance that also favors the smaller bases under the assumption of no cannibalization.

In this sense, DRIVE can be said to favor smaller bases. But the story is not quite complete. Figure 7.2 portrays the same case as Figure 7.1 but with the assumption of full cannibalization in the evaluation, the same assumption made in DRIVE's optimization algorithm. Please note the change in scale in Figure 7.2. It only shows the 90–100 percent availability range to emphasize the differ-

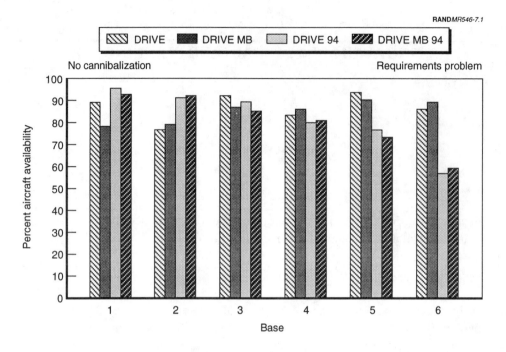

Figure 7.1—How a Lower Aircraft Availability Goal Affects DRIVE's Performance Without Cannibalization

ences between the heights of the various bars, all of which are between 91 and 97 percent. The heights of the two rightmost bars at each base reflect a dramatic improvement compared to the case where no cannibalization is assumed. Note, too, the remarkably similar performance at every base delivered by the stock levels allocated by the minimum base version of DRIVE. The difference in aircraft availability between the highest and lowest base is only 0.62 percent of possessed aircraft. Clearly, cannibalization benefits the larger base more than the smaller one.

Cannibalization has a powerful effect on system performance and, because it is explicitly accounted for in DRIVE's optimization procedure, it results in a significant shift in stock levels in favor of the smaller base when aircraft availability goals are specified to be less than 100 percent. This is why performance at the larger bases is so poor under the assumption of no cannibalization.

Figure 7.3 reflects the numbers of LRUs allocated to each base by DRIVE, DRIVE with 94 percent goals (DRIVE 94), and DRIVE with 88 percent goals (DRIVE 88), which allows 2, 4, and 8 aircraft down at the 18-, 36-, and 72-PAA bases, respectively, twice as many in each case as the 94 percent goal. Note the dramatic shift in the allocations as the goals are reduced.

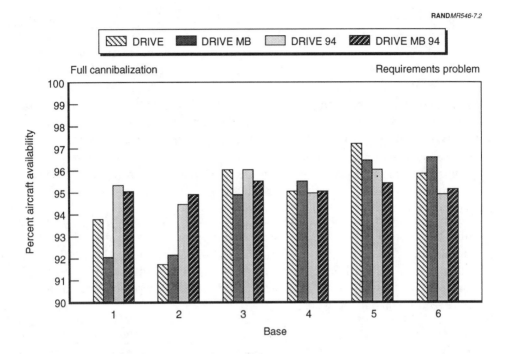

Figure 7.2—Cannibalization Makes a Big Difference

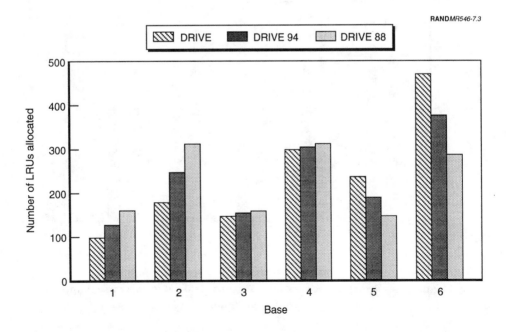

Figure 7.3—Reducing DRIVE's Goals Induces Dramatic Reallocations of LRUs

Although it is true that the larger bases benefit more from cannibalization than the smaller ones, it is also true that, in the face of the shift in allocations associated with reduced goals, system performance depends more heavily on cannibalization. Especially striking is the fact that, with 88 percent goals, DRIVE actually allocated more LRUs to the 18-PAA bases than it did to the 72-PAA bases, hardly an intuitively appealing outcome. But this is a natural result of the full cannibalization assumption. The policy issue underlying the use of any model that assumes full cannibalization deserves very careful and sober consideration of the costs involved in maintenance manhours and component wear-and-tear. Results such as the ones shown in Figure 7.3 make one wonder about the wisdom of such a policy.

The results shown in Figure 7.2 seem very satisfying, especially for the minimum-base version of DRIVE, except for the fact that, when we specified 88 percent aircraft availability goals at all the bases (allowing 2, 4, and 8 aircraft down at the 18-, 36-, and 72-PAA bases, respectively), the results were not as good. Figure 7.4 portrays the evaluative results under the assumption of no cannibalization for the 88 percent goals.

RAND*MR546-7.4*

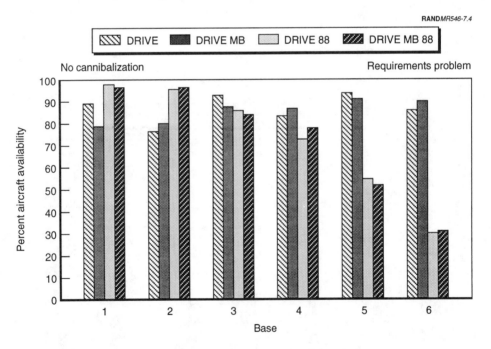

Figure 7.4—Reducing the Goal to 88 Percent Makes Matters Worse Without Cannibalization

In Figure 7.5, we portray the results of the same evaluations under the assumption of full cannibalization. Again, we point out the change in the vertical scale in Figure 7.5. The performance of the minimum-base version of DRIVE isn't quite as constant among the bases as in the 94 percent case. The difference among the highest and lowest base availability here is 3.05 percent of possessed aircraft, roughly five times as great as in the 94 percent case, although still fairly modest compared to the unconstrained DRIVE.

SPECIFYING THE GOALS TO DRIVE IN EXECUTION

These results led us to examine the role of the aircraft availability goal specified to DRIVE in execution in Dyna-METRIC. The results shown in Figures 7.4 and 7.5 resulted from the specification of a goal of 88 percent to DRIVE in execution, a goal consistent with the goal used to determine the stock levels in the requirements problem. Further analysis of this phenomenon led to the interesting and important result that the aircraft availability goals specified to DRIVE in execution in Dyna-METRIC also play a role in shaping performance with goals less than 100 percent.

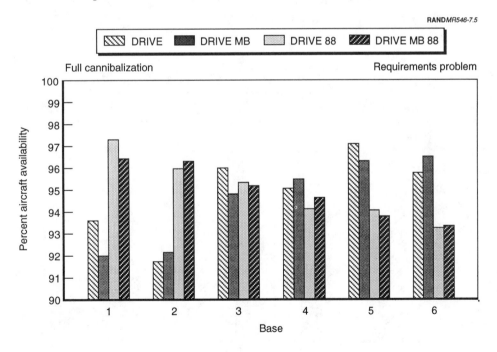

Figure 7.5—The 88 Percent Case with Full Cannibalization

Figure 7.6 reflects the results of full-cannibalization evaluations of the minimum-base DRIVE with 88 percent goals, where we specified 88 percent goals to DRIVE in execution in Dyna-METRIC in one case (DRIVE MB 88/88) and 100 percent in the other case (DRIVE MB 88/100). Again, please make special note of the vertical scale. The difference in aircraft availability between the highest and lowest base has been reduced from 3.05 to only 0.85 percent of possessed aircraft. Full cannibalization and the specification of 100 percent availability goals to DRIVE in execution in Dyna-METRIC have eliminated the poorer performance at the larger bases of the stock levels determined by the minimum base version of DRIVE with 88 percent goals noted in Figure 7.4. They have, in fact, minimized both the base-size and weapon-system effects very nicely.

Another anomaly resulted from the evaluations of DRIVE using a 94 percent aircraft availability goal in the requirements problem with a 100 percent goal specified to DRIVE in execution in Dyna-METRIC. In the case of DRIVE MB 88/100, the uniformity among observed base availability rates improved over the DRIVE MB 88/88 case. In the 94 percent case, the specification of 100 percent goals to DRIVE in execution in Dyna-METRIC had just the opposite effect. We do not understand this phenomenon. Additional research and evaluation are needed to understand this behavior better. The results for the 94 percent case are shown in Figure 7.7.

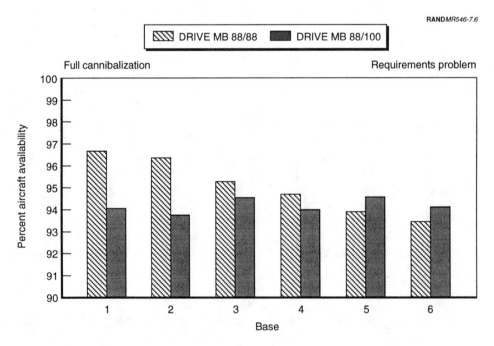

Figure 7.6—DRIVE's Goals in Execution Are Important to Performance

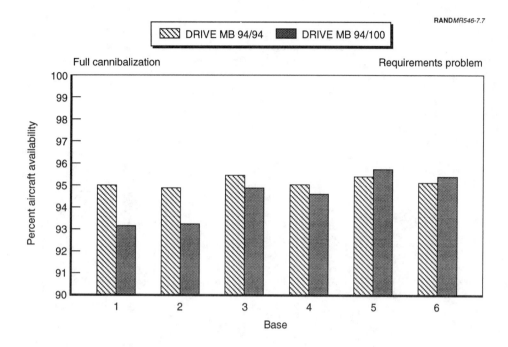

Figure 7.7—A Different Effect in the 94 Percent Case

In Figure 7.8, we compare the performance of the minimum base version of DRIVE using 94 percent goals (DRIVE MB 94) with those of METRIC and the minimum base version of the AAM (AAM MB) under the assumption of full cannibalization. The most heterogeneous performance of these three is delivered by METRIC, the most homogeneous by DRIVE MB with the 94 percent goals. The AAM MB does not deliver as homogeneous a performance under full cannibalization as it does under the assumption of no cannibalization. This is not surprising, since it assumes no cannibalization in its optimization procedure. DRIVE MB does better in this sense under full cannibalization, again because the cannibalization assumption made in the evaluation is consistent with the assumption made in optimization.

Another important lesson emerges from this work. The procedure used in the requirements problem should incorporate the most realistic possible assumptions, i.e., the assumptions most consistent with the behavior of the system in the real world. If cannibalization, lateral supply, or other management adaptation is routinely practiced in the real world, it should be assumed in the model (Abell et al., 1993).

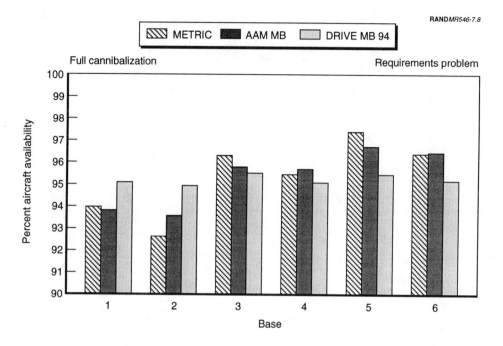

Figure 7.8—Full Cannibalization Evaluations of METRIC, AAM MB, and DRIVE MB 94

DETERMINING THE PLANNING HORIZONS TO USE IN DRIVE

Like the aircraft availability goals one specifies to DRIVE in the requirements problem or to DRIVE in execution, the planning horizon specified to DRIVE in the requirements problem also has an important effect on system performance. The means of the probability density functions that estimate the demands at each base during the planning horizon are, of course, strictly linear functions of the planning horizon lengths. Their specified numerical values have substantial effects on the mix of stock levels determined in the requirements problem.

In a variation of the scenario we have discussed at length, which had a 20-day retrograde time, we changed the retrograde time to 2 days to agree with the order-and-ship time and more closely represent a "lean logistics" concept of operations. Thus, with no depot stock, the delay time the base sees in submitting a requisition is the order-and-ship time (2 days) plus the retrograde time (2 days) plus the administrative handling time (1 day) plus the on-stand repair time (1 day) plus queuing time (say 1 day), a total of about 7 days depot repair cycle time. All of the evaluations of DRIVE in the scenario previously discussed (with the 20-day retrograde time) used a 30-day planning horizon in both stock leveling and execution.

In our initial evaluations of alternative approaches to the requirements problem in the revised scenario (with the 2-day retrograde time), we found that METRIC's stock levels performed substantially better than DRIVE's did. Subsequent analysis showed why: the mix of stock levels produced by the two approaches, DRIVE with a 30-day planning horizon and METRIC, were very different. After additional evaluations, we concluded that, in determining stock levels, DRIVE should be used with a planning horizon equal to the total depot repair cycle time and, as before, should have the expected number of assets in base repair added to the expected demands at each base. The result of this approach is a set of probability density functions that are similar to those used by METRIC; they transform DRIVE into a pipeline model of sorts.

The leftmost two bars at each base in Figure 7.9 show the performance of stock levels determined by DRIVE with a 30-day planning horizon (DRIVE 30) and those of METRIC. The rightmost two bars at each base demonstrate the effects of specifying the planning horizon in a way that more closely approximates the pipeline, using a 10-day horizon in one case and a 7-day horizon in the other. DRIVE with a 30-day planning horizon delivers almost 7 percent less worldwide aircraft availability than METRIC, but DRIVE with a 7-day planning horizon re-

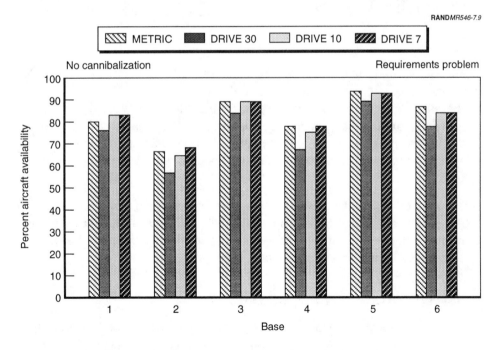

RAND*MR546-7.9*

Figure 7.9—Planning Horizon Specification Has Significant Effects

duces that difference to only 0.6 percent. (All of these evaluations were done with a 30-day planning horizon specified to DRIVE in execution in Dyna-METRIC.)

Figure 7.10 shows the stock level allocations to the six bases determined by DRIVE with a 30-day planning horizon, DRIVE with a 5-day planning horizon, and METRIC in the scenario with the 2-day retrograde time. Note that DRIVE with a 30-day horizon allocates too few stock levels to the smaller bases and too many to the larger ones relative to DRIVE with a 7-day horizon and METRIC with no depot stock, whose allocations are, in fact, identical.

SPECIFYING THE PLANNING HORIZON IN EXECUTION

System performance is much less sensitive to planning horizon specification in DRIVE in execution than to DRIVE in stock leveling. The difference in world-wide aircraft availability between a 5-day planning horizon in execution versus a 30-day horizon is only 0.19 percent of possessed aircraft. We conclude that, for the sake of consistency between DRIVE's recommended asset allocations and base due-ins, the original issue of interest here, DRIVE's planning horizon in execution should be set equal to

$$NRTS(TDRCT + OST) + (1 - NRTS)BRT,$$

where $NRTS$ is defined to be the NRTS rate expressed as a decimal fraction, BRT is the base repair time, OST is the order-and-ship time, and $TDRCT$ is defined to be the total depot repair cycle time. $TDRCT$ includes retrograde time plus the total average time an asset spends in the hands of the depot. That should include processing time, repair time, queuing time, packing and crating time, delay time, etc., but should not include time spent in reparable storage awaiting induction.

This guidance differs from the guidance in our original documentation of DRIVE (Abell et al., 1992; Miller and Abell, 1992), but represents our best judgment about the performance of DRIVE's stock levels and the need for consistency between asset allocations and base due-ins.

SENSITIVITY TO DEPOT REPAIR TIME

In a system without depot stock, one might conjecture that DRIVE's contribution to depot responsiveness and system performance might be inhibited if depot repair times were longer than those specified in these evaluations (1 day on-stand time and 1 day administrative handling time). Evaluations demonstrated that this is not the case. Changing the on-stand time from 1 day to as much as

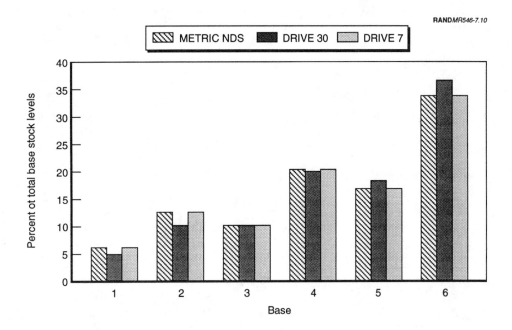

Figure 7.10—The Effects of Planning Horizon Length on the Distribution of DRIVE's Stock Levels Among Bases

20 days affected worldwide availability less than one-half of one percent. We conclude that system performance with DRIVE in execution is very robust with respect to depot repair times.

Chapter Eight

CONCLUSIONS AND RECOMMENDATIONS

CONCLUSIONS

In the next several paragraphs we summarize our observations and conclusions in this body of research.

As we have shown, approaches that optimize worldwide objective functions may yield very different levels of performance for individual bases and weapon systems. That fact should not be overlooked in goal setting. To achieve the balance in performance desired among bases and weapon systems, additional constraints may be needed in the optimization procedure being used. The minimum base versions of the models we evaluated in this research are intended only to be illustrative of the kinds of enhancements that may be more attractive to policymakers than the standard versions of the models.

As we previously pointed out, the solution to the requirements problem has far more leverage over system performance than does the solution to the pure stock leveling problem. Recall that our definitions of the requirements problem and the stock leveling problem are quite restrictive. When one suggests setting stock levels with a particular approach, one is probably talking about what we have termed the requirements problem. Any time we determine the richness of stock levels in the system, we are solving the problem we have defined here as the requirements problem. The stock leveling problem, remember, is constrained to use a predefined mix of assets that predetermines the sum of stock levels of each type asset to be allocated.

It is also important to realize that the actual stock leveling problem one faces in the real world is a hybrid of the requirements problem and the pure stock leveling problem. Sometimes, when there are ample assets of a particular type in the inventory system, the stock leveling system determines the level of richness of that item to be reflected in the stock levels. For other items, it solves only the pure stock leveling problem because it runs out of assets before it reaches the desired level of richness.

It is important that stock levels be determined with the same approach and assumptions used to prioritize repairs and allocate assets to achieve consistency between asset allocations and base due-ins. Although this is, in a sense, an administrative issue, it is an important one both for system performance (we don't want needed asset allocations to be inhibited by lack of a requisition) and for bases' perceptions of depot performance (we don't want unfilled requisitions to wait for prolonged periods in the depot backorder file).

As we have seen, METRIC is a tough act to follow. It generally performs best in worldwide measures, at least for LRUs, but perhaps not in an entirely satisfying way for individual bases and weapon systems. Since the Aircraft Availability Model accounts explicitly for weapon system differences in its peripheral software that enables a decisionmaker to specify goals for individual weapon systems, it is a sensible approach, especially if it is constrained to deal with the base size effect. It clearly has the right objective function, although its assumption of random shortages among aircraft is not always realistic. DRIVE is a sensible approach as well, but has a somewhat troublesome objective function.

As a decision support system in execution, DRIVE helps achieve good performance, but its contribution is less important when the system has depot stock than when all the stock is allocated to the bases. It is especially important in achieving responsive depot repair when no stock is allocated to the depot.

We conclude that DRIVE is the best choice for stock leveling, but only if it is used to prioritize repairs and allocate assets. It performs about as well as other optimization approaches, especially in the presence of cannibalization.

Using DRIVE to set stock levels simply extends the same logic used for repair requirements determination, repair prioritization, and asset allocation to the stock leveling problem. This consistency resolves the logical issue of "push" versus "pull," i.e., requisitions and stock levels versus asset positions and aircraft availability goals, and the original issue that motivated this research, i.e., that asset allocations did not always match base due-ins. Having said this, however, we hasten to add that additional research and evaluation are needed to understand how goal setting, for both stock leveling and execution, affects system performance. It has important implications for models that incorporate cannibalization assumptions. The planning horizon specified to DRIVE in stock leveling is important in shaping system performance. The method suggested in Chapter Seven seems to yield the best performance over a wide range of conditions and, although system performance is much less sensitive to the planning horizon length in execution, it should be specified in the same way, again for the sake of consistency between base due-ins and asset allocations.

We would like to see the choice of stock leveling algorithm made in full light of its performance with SRUs included, because DRIVE has arguably the best model of LRU-SRU failure relationships of any of those evaluated. Our past evaluations of DRIVE suggest that much of DRIVE's improved effectiveness over that of the current system derives from its surgical allocations of SRUs and its explicit model of SRU failures. Unfortunately, because we excluded SRUs from these evaluations in the interests of time and simplicity, our results probably underestimate DRIVE's performance relative to the other approaches, especially that of METRIC, which treats LRUs and SRUs indistinguishably. Thus, there is no reason to delay the application of DRIVE to central stock leveling for assets for which it is being used in execution.

The logical choice of decision support environment for stock leveling is clearly Desktop DRIVE. Its database is sufficient for the task and is updated very frequently (daily in its application at Ogden). The desktop environment enables human participation in resource allocation decisionmaking much better in contrast to a monolithic sort of centralized system operating at AFMC Headquarters. The person who operates Desktop DRIVE for a manageable workload is able to contact item managers, equipment specialists, or shop chiefs to resolve data discrepancies and other problems conveniently, face-to-face if necessary, thus providing some sanity checks of allocation decisions made by the computerized algorithm.

What is ultimately needed is a modification to DRIVE that will incorporate an expected aircraft availability objective function and retain the power of its sort values, POS-RSP tradeoff ability, SRU failure model, base-specific treatment of aircraft availability goals, and frequent, responsive operation to stay closely attuned to the evolving asset position.

RECOMMENDATIONS

Our recommendations are few and straightforward. First, we recommend the use of DRIVE for central stock leveling, but only when DRIVE is used in repair prioritization and asset allocation. It should be implemented using Desktop DRIVE, and its use should be demonstrated in stock leveling at Ogden for F-16 avionics components.

The use of the SBSS and negotiated stock levels should be avoided whenever possible. D028 is, in principle, a superior method of setting stock levels. When DRIVE is not used in execution, D028 may be the approach of choice. The problems inhibiting the use of D028 should be resolved and it should be made fully operational again.

This research should be extended to include SRUs. Moreover, additional research is needed in setting aircraft availability goals with DRIVE, both in stock leveling and in execution, and should include extensive evaluations of system performance, especially when DRIVE is used to set differential goals. Incorporation of an expected aircraft availability objective function in DRIVE should also be fully developed.

A REPRESENTATION OF DRIVE IN DYNA-METRIC

Since we used Dyna-METRIC as an evaluation tool and consistency between planning and execution is the primary motivation for this research, it was necessary to endow Dyna-METRIC with the ability to operate according to DRIVE priorities. This appendix describes how this was done.

OVERVIEW

In addition to ignoring SRUs, this interpretation differs from "real" DRIVE in that it is much more real-time. Rather than make repair and distribution priority lists intended to hold over significant production periods, priorities are indicated by data structures that are consulted and updated whenever an event requiring a decision occurs. There are three kinds of such events: the receipt of a requisition, implying that the asset position of an LRU at a base has changed; the arrival of an LRU carcass at the depot, making it available for repair; and the completion of a repair, indicating that there is an LRU to be allocated and that the test stand involved can start a new repair. Beyond initialization of the DRIVE database, the rest of the Dyna-METRIC program interacts with DRIVE only through calls to these three event routines. In order to further isolate the representation of DRIVE from the rest of the simulation, the DRIVE portion maintains its own database of status information (asset positions, queues, and what test stands are doing).

TEST STAND AND ALLOCATION "LISTS"

DRIVE maintains two data structures called the TS (Test Stand) and AL (Allocation) lists.[1] There is a TS list for every kind of test stand and an AL list for

---

[1] "List" in this context is used in the sense of list processing in programming, examples of which are "sets" in SIMSCRIPT and "queue objects" in MODSIM. A list, or more properly "queue," is a group of records ("members") that are chained together and ordered through forward and backward

every kind of LRU. Member records on either type of list are associated with LRU-base pairs (e.g., LRU number 3 and base number 7), and an LRU-base is represented by at most one record on either kind of list. The records on any list are ordered by the current sort values associated with allocating an additional LRU to the base. When a decision is needed regarding the allocation of an LRU, the first record on the LRU's AL list is consulted. Likewise, when a test stand becomes available, the LRU indicated by the first record on the test stand's list is chosen to begin repair. The real-time aspect of DRIVE is achieved by keeping all the lists up to date as events occur.

There are two reasons for having two separate kinds of lists. Real DRIVE (or at least the Ogden Prototype) makes a single list that is later separated into repair lists and distribution lists. The TS and AL lists correspond to these. The second reason is more complex. For a particular LRU-base pair, the sort values used to rank lists are usually the same for the AL and TS lists. When an LRU goes onto a test stand (because it is the LRU specified in the first record on the LRU's applicable TS list), the sort value of the record is degraded and the record is moved in the TS list accordingly. This constitutes an assumption that the base involved is going to get the LRU when the repair is completed. Now the sort values in the two lists will be different, with the one in the AL list being greater. This provides a way of indicating that the repair is being taken care of and still allows the base to be in contention for more LRUs of the same type. When a repair is completed, the allocation of the LRU is done by consulting the LRU's AL list. A specific test stand knows the base for which it thought it was doing the repair when the repair action began. If that base is not the base that gets the LRU, then the disappointed base gets its TS list priority for the LRU upgraded.

EVENTS

As mentioned previously, there are three kinds of events that trigger decisions: receipt of a requisition, arrival of a carcass at the depot, and completion of a repair. We describe each of these events at greater length in the discussion that follows.

Receipt of a Requisition

The requisition procedure, called requisitionEvent in the code, is provided indices of the LRU and base involved in sending the requisition. This is DRIVE's notification that a base's asset position has degraded. In processing the event, a check is made to see if there is depot stock. If so, as far as DRIVE is concerned,

---

pointers that are fields within the records. A list also has an "owner" with variables pointing to the first and last records. Lists are used both to group things and to order them by some attribute.

an LRU will be sent and there is no change in the base's asset position. If there are no LRUs available, DRIVE adjusts its view of the base's asset position and calls for the updating of both the AL and TS lists. The header for the requisition event (in Pascal syntax; var indicates a value to be returned) is

```
procedure requisitionEvent( lru, base : integer; var gotSent : boolean );
```

where the first two arguments identify the two entities involved. The boolean (logical) variable, gotSent, is returned to inform the caller whether or not the requisition was filled from depot stock.

Carcass Arrival

This event, encoded in a procedure named carcArrival, notifies DRIVE that an LRU carcass is available for repair. Assuming that Dyna-METRIC would model depot repair as an administrative delay followed by entrance into a (multichannel) queuing system, carcArrival would be invoked at the completion of the administrative delay. The procedure tallies the new arrival and looks to see if the appropriate type of test stand has a free server. If there is a free server, carcArrival calls upon the procedure findJob, which returns the index of the base most in need of the LRU. Then carcArrival finds the specific server and invokes the startWork procedure. The procedure's header is

```
procedure carcArrival( lru : integer; var ts, server, base : integer );
```

where the first argument indicates to the procedure what kind of LRU is involved, and the next two (ts and server) would inform the caller which server on what kind of test stand has become engaged. The base indicator is for DRIVE's use in updating the TS list. If the repair of the LRU cannot be started, all three arguments are returned with zeros. If work can be started, the TS list is updated by the call to startWork.

Completion of a Repair

This procedure is invoked when Dyna-METRIC determines that the repair of an LRU has been completed. Its job is to see to the allocation of the LRU, and either find something else for the server to do or note that the server is idle. The header is

```
procedure repairComplete( ts, server : integer; var allocLRU, allocBase,
                          startLRU : integer );
```

where the test stand type and server indicate which resource just completed a repair. The returned values allocLRU and allocBase are to inform the caller about what LRU was repaired and to whom DRIVE wants to send it. The last argument, startLRU, tells the caller what kind of LRU is now to go on the test stand if an appropriate carcass is available. It may be that the allocation list for the LRU just repaired is empty, in which case allocBase will be zero, from which Dyna-METRIC infers that the LRU be put into the depot's stock. If there is no carcass available to put on the test stand, startLRU will come back as zero.

This procedure updates the TS and AL lists in several ways. If the LRU is allocated to a base, both lists are modified. If the base for which the repair was started is not the base that gets the LRU, then its priority in the TS list is upgraded. Finally, if there is another LRU whose repair can be started (identified through a call to findJob) the invocation of startWork will update the lists.

PROCEDURES

The hierarchy of procedures is shown in Figure A.1.

RUNNING DYNA-METRIC WITH DRIVE

Since we have specific and limited uses for simulation, the integration of DRIVE into Dyna-METRIC is not as complete as every possible user could want. The following conditions apply:

- DRIVE is specified by including an option (OPT) 34 record.

- The planning horizon is specified by the second parameter on the option 11 record.

- Depot distribution policy (column 79 on the second record) and depot scheduling policy (column 5 on TBED records) are ignored.

- A number of servers for each depot repair resource should be specified on TBED records, and all LRUs need to be assigned to a (constrained) repair resource on a TPRT record. (This is unlike normal Dyna-METRIC, where unassigned parts are treated as though they are repaired with unconstrained resources.)

- Only two echelons of repair are allowed: base and depot, and the run should not include SRUs.

- In compiling, the DMLSTMAX parameter in the file dimen.for is no longer set to 1. It should be at least DMSTANDS times DMTEQTYP, as it is now used to dimension some of the DRIVE variables.

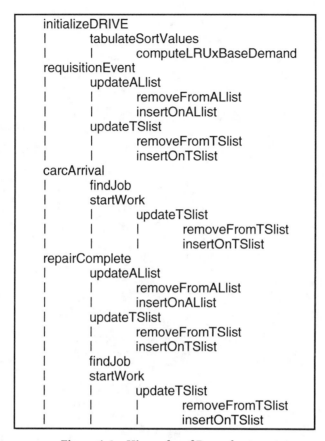

```
initializeDRIVE
|        tabulateSortValues
|        |        computeLRUxBaseDemand
requisitionEvent
|        updateALlist
|        |        removeFromALlist
|        |        insertOnALlist
|        updateTSlist
|        |        removeFromTSlist
|        |        insertOnTSlist
carcArrival
|        findJob
|        startWork
|        |        updateTSlist
|        |        |        removeFromTSlist
|        |        |        insertOnTSlist
repairComplete
|        updateALlist
|        |        removeFromALlist
|        |        insertOnALlist
|        updateTSlist
|        |        removeFromTSlist
|        |        insertOnTSlist
|        findJob
|        startWork
|        |        updateTSlist
|        |        |        removeFromTSlist
|        |        |        insertOnTSlist
```

Figure A.1—Hierarchy of Procedures

Abell, John B., Louis W. Miller, Curtis E. Neumann, and Judith E. Payne, *DRIVE (Distribution and Repair in Variable Environments): Enhancing the Responsiveness of Depot Repair*, Santa Monica, Calif.: RAND, R-3888-AF, 1992.

Abell, John B., Grace M. Carter, Karen E. Isaacson, and Thomas F. Lippiatt, *Estimating Requirements for Aircraft Recoverable Spares and Depot Repair*, Santa Monica, Calif.: RAND, R-4210-AF, 1993.

Culosi, Salvatore J., and Frank L. Eichorn, *A Comparison of Two Systems for Distributing Spare Parts*, Bethesda, Md.: Logistics Management Institute, LMI Report AS201R1, March 1993.

Dynamics Research Corporation, *WSMIS Distribution and Repair in Variable Environments Module (DRIVE, DO87J/K) Functional Description, Version 2.4*, Andover, Mass.: E-1622U, April 1994.

Hanks, Christopher H., and R. C. Kline, *Assets vs. Requirements: Why Asset-Based Central Leveling Is a Good Idea*, Bethesda, Md.: Logistics Management Institute, LMI Report AF601R4, August 1987.

Isaacson, Karen E., and Patricia M. Boren, *Dyna-METRIC Version 6: An Advanced Capability Assessment Model*, Santa Monica, Calif.: RAND, R-4214-AF, 1993.

Miller, Bruce L., *A Real Time METRIC for the Distribution of Serviceable Assets*, Santa Monica, Calif.: RAND, RM-5687-PR, October 1968.

Miller, Louis W., and John B. Abell, *DRIVE (Distribution and Repair in Variable Environments): Design and Operation of the Ogden Prototype*, Santa Monica, Calif.: RAND, R-4158-AF, 1992.

For more information or to order RAND documents, see RAND's URL: http://www.rand.org/ RAND documents may also be ordered via the Internet: order@rand.org/

Muckstadt, J., "A Model for a Multi-Item, Multi-Echelon, Multi-Indenture Inventory System," *Management Science*, Vol. 20, 1973, pp. 472–481.

O'Malley, T. J., *The Aircraft Availability Model: Conceptual Framework and Mathematics*, Bethesda, Md.: Logistics Management Institute, 1983.

Palm, C., "Analysis of the Erlang Traffic Formula for Busy-Signal Arrangements," *Ericsson Technics*, No. 5, 1938, pp. 39–58.

Sherbrooke, Craig C., "METRIC: A Multi-Echelon Technique for Recoverable Item Control," *Operations Research*, Vol. 16, 1968, pp. 122–141.

Sherbrooke, Craig C., *Estimation of the Variance-to-Mean Ratio for AFLC Recoverable items*, Potomac, Md.: Sherbrooke and Associates, January 1984.

Sherbrooke, Craig C., "VARI-METRIC: Improved Approximations for Multi-Indenture, Multi-Echelon Availability Models," *Operations Research*, Vol. 34, 1986, pp. 311–319.

Sherbrooke, Craig C., *Optimal Inventory Modeling of Systems: Multi-Echelon Techniques*, New York: John Wiley & Sons, Inc., 1992.

Simon, R. M., "Stationary Properties of a Two-Echelon Inventory Model for Low-Demand Items," *Operations Research*, Vol. 19, 1971, pp. 761–773.